"It is my pleasure to recommend Richard T. Young's delightful and insightful text on the creation of Oral Interpretation performance. Professor Young introduces his text with a meaningful and entertaining definition of art, which he accurately points out is work that is created by human design. He distinguishes the art of Oral Interpretation from other forms of communication such as public speaking and acting. He describes various forms of material that are suitable for interpretation to audiences of all types. He describes the art of individual and choral performances, sprinkled with personal anecdotes from his classroom and professional work. He provides a multitude of techniques and exercises for teaching Oral Interpretation that are indispensable. All in all, I found this to be an entertaining, highly professional, and thoroughly enjoyable text on how to teach Oral Interpretation that every teacher of the subject should consider using."

—**Edward Emanuel,** Professor Emeritus, Department of Theater Arts, California State University-Fresno

"Starting with a cogent definition of art (no easy task!), Richard T. Young systematically walks both teacher and student through the crucial elements involved in the performing art of Oral Interpretation. From aesthetics to technique, with examples, exercises, anecdotes, and an articulate passion for the material, this exhaustive text is the new definitive teaching tool that is a must in every Oral Interpretation curriculum."

—**John Wilson,** Professor, Actor, and author of *The Actor as Fire and Cloud*

"In this refreshing book, master teacher, director, and performer Richard T. Young has crafted a practical, readable book on the art of oral interpretation. Young covers the step-by-step approach to make texts come to life, while also offering the reader the deeper meaning of embodying a written text for audience appreciation and enjoyment. This book is perfect for teachers and lovers of literature who wish to represent the texts they love for audiences everywhere."

—**Elizabeth W. McLaughlin,** Professor of Communication, Bethel University, Indiana

Oral Interpretation

Oral Interpretation

A Creative Performance Approach

RICHARD T. YOUNG

Integratio Press

Pasco, Washington

This is a publication of Trinity House, a Division of Integratio Press

integratiopress.com

Integratio Press is an Imprint of Christianity and Communication Studies Network
11503 Easton Dr.
Pasco, WA 99301

www.theccsn.com

Cover design: Carol O'Callaghan
Interior design: Atritex Technologies
Image: Depositphotos

paperback isbn: 978-1-959685-19-7
ebook isbn: 978-1-959685-20-3

Library of Congress Control Number: 2024946482

Dedication

This text is dedicated to oral interpretation teachers everywhere who know how to make it fun.

Table of Contents

Acknowledgments

PROFESSOR NOBLE JOHNSON, THANK YOU for teaching/leading us into the riotous fun of oral interpretation. To my colleagues at Blackburn College, I say thank you for the sabbatical which allowed for the first draft of this text to be written.

Chapter 1

Destination Unknown

Oral Interpretation—A Performing Art

WHAT IS ART? THIS IS A QUESTION we, as teachers and students, can begin to answer, even if that answer will never be complete or absolutely accurate.

In my Introduction to Theater course, my students and I spend several days in discussion trying to define art. I do what all good college professors do: I make them write out their definitions as a starting place for our discussion. Frequently they assert, and with some vigor, "Everything is art, and art is everything." *This is an easy answer, and it is a wrong answer.*

Certainly, there are aesthetic aspects to everything. But it is a mistake to equate beauty, or form, or activity with art. A sunset can be amazing in its color. To stand at the edge of the Grand Canyon is to stand at the edge of grandeur. A giraffe silhouetted by the setting sun on the great plains of Africa is beyond the definition of beauty. And while all those things embody beauty and truth and wonderment, they are not art. If a human being has not purposefully manipulated it, then it is not art.

At the very least, for something to be art it must be touched by human hands. Suppose I take a picture of the silhouetted giraffe. That picture may now qualify as art. I interjected my viewpoint into what is saved for others to see. The giraffe moves on, the sun goes down, but I saved the moment. I saved the beauty. I turned a wonderful, naturally occurring vision into art.

Some have suggested to me that this idea denigrates the meaning of art. I say no. If I said for something to possess beauty it must be manipulated by humankind, then that surely, would denigrate the meaning of beauty. Beauty occurs naturally without the assistance of humans; art does not.

Successful Art Causes Us to Ponder

Some things are obviously art; others are not. Take for instance a plastic garbage bag full of trash. That bag, in and of itself, is not art. But twice I have seen full-sized sculptures of garbage-filled trash bags—one in white stone, the other in black metal. Each had the wrinkles, bulges, folds, and look of a real trash bag. They were amazingly well-detailed sculptures. They were art.

If someone puts a real garbage bag full of real garbage on display in an art gallery is it art? Art such as this real-trash-bag-on-display does exist. I was at a gallery opening where one of the "works of art" was a piece of hard asphalt construction material that the artist had not manipulated in any way other than to pick it up off the ground and put it on display. I asked the artist why this was no longer trash and was now art. He talked to me for a long time about aesthetics and beauty and relevance, but he did not answer the question. He *did* cause me to take a moment to look at a piece of construction debris that otherwise I would not have given a first glance. In other words, the only reason I looked at it was because it was part of an art show. Perhaps, therein, lies a fraction of our answer to the question, "What is art?"

Michelangelo's *David* is art, and no sane person would disagree. The *David* is an astounding piece—visually arresting! Even though I had seen pictures, I was not prepared for the effect that seeing the *David* in real time and space had on me. The sculpture literally grips your attention. It forces the onlooker to truly look. This phenomenon is confirmed by simply watching those who study the *David*. As I sat and watched, I could see awe on face after face. Theatrical genius and director Peter Brook writes about theater causing us to look at life in a very concentrated way. He proposes that theater makes us look intently at a moment, or a thought, or an idea. Perhaps Brook leads us to a definition, or at least a partial definition of art.

Art is a moment of life, an idea, a thought, an image, an object, or anything that is purposefully presented in such a way as to say to an observer, "Come ponder this." The stone and metal sculptures of a garbage bag, the *David*, and the construction debris all succeeded in causing the viewers to examine them specifically. The artists behind these works succeeded in causing people to pause and look at the piece in an aesthetic way.

One measure of the success of art is the degree or depth of pondering it garners from those who view it. I remember the *David* well. I remember the white stone sculpture of a garbage bag. But more than their appearance,

I remember how I felt when I saw them. I remember how I thought they were truly amazing, and how I studied them for a long time. I remember the black metal sculpture of the garbage bag, but it is a fuzzy memory, and the same is true for the construction debris. I probably only remember the construction debris because it was an example of "found" art, rather than something that was created. Neither of the latter two caused me to "ponder" them as much as the first two.

The meaning of the word "ponder" is important to this definition of art. According to the thesaurus, synonyms for ponder include "consider," "reflect," "contemplate," "meditate," "think," and "muse." The antonym for ponder is "forget."

Successful art leaves us with an impression that lingers in our hearts and minds. I recall an old farmer telling me, "I thought about that play all the next day." He had come to see a performance of *Godspell* I had directed for a church. I do not think he had seen much theater before, and we successfully caused him to ponder.

For something to be *art*, a human being must have somehow manipulated it. For something to be art, it must also cause those who experience it to ponder. The intensity of that pondering can be an indication of how good, wonderful, or excellent that art is.

Oral Interpretation Is One of the Performing Arts

My first exposure to oral interpretation was in the fifth grade. Our teacher, Mr. K, told us we would prepare a performance for the school's Christmas show, and we all would participate. The next day we began rehearsal on a choral reader's version of the *Twelve Days of Christmas*. Mr. K stood in front and directed us throughout the rehearsal process. Using hand gestures, he directed us to be louder or softer, faster or slower, pause and resume. He added in some special touches, such as having only five voices call out the line "five golden rings," and we made various sounds to go along with "swans a swimming," "maids a milking," and "drummers drumming."

It was so much fun we took our scripts with us to recess and practiced on our own. Judging by the audience response, our performance was a success. As I recall, Mr. K took a flamboyant bow as our parents applauded. He never called our performance "oral interpretation," much less "choral reading," but that is what it was.

My next encounter with oral interpretation was in my high school writers' club. Once a week we gathered and read our latest works aloud. Of course, we did not just read them; we performed them. I felt an incredible thrill when my clubmates gave me a standing ovation after I read my poem "Only the Pelicans Came." And I tried hard not to shed tears as Classmate P read us her poem about the kitty that had been hit by a car. She read *Kitty* at almost every meeting, by request. We were writers and we liked to feel deeply. While we did not recognize these readings as such, we were seriously engaged in oral interpretation.

As a sophomore in college, I enrolled in an oral interpretation course. Professor J had us perform all the classic forms of literature: poetry, fiction, nonfiction, and drama. He also let us explore any other form of written work we wanted. I cannot say all our choices qualified as literature, since one performance was of a soup can label.

I took an upper-division oral interpretation course from Doctor H. I remember her glasses hanging off the end of her nose as she cracked her chewing gum and encouraged us to "experiment" with the piece. She formed us into small groups with the assignment of creating a ten-minute long reader's theater as our final project. My two partners and I chose the work of a contemporary American writer who was a cross between a poet and an essay writer. We were not very creative, and we did not rehearse well. Our performance was mediocre at best, and some of our classmates had far more polished and entertaining shows.

I took a reader's theater workshop from Doctor C. We created an hour-long performance called "We Like It Here, But." The theme was the fortes and foibles of America, and our compiled script included everything from *MAD* magazine to the Declaration of Independence. We covered American history from Custer's last stand to the topless dancer Carol Doda. We juxtaposed somber and silly moments.

In graduate school I enrolled in a reader's theater workshop with Doctor E. We recorded Shakespeare on tape for the blind. That class was the only time I ever got to perform some of the great roles in Shakespeare.

Since graduate school, I have performed oral interpretations in church, in my classes, at conferences, seminars, and fundraising gatherings for local arts organizations. I have directed reader's theaters in all those venues. Along the way I have seen many other reader's theaters, judged oral interpretation performances at high school speech contests, and been in a couple of oral interpretation contests myself.

I include this long recitation of my experience with oral interpretation to bring us to a simple conclusion: *Oral interpretation is one of the performing arts.*

- Oral interpretation is more than a classroom exercise. It is certainly a valuable classroom exercise for many reasons that I will explore later. But at the same time, it is much more.

- Oral interpretation is not just a way to explore literature. While it is that, and there are books devoted to oral interpretation as a form of exploring literature, it is much more than exploring literature. Oral interpretation is the presentation of literature, and it is more than the literature itself.

- Oral interpretation is not simply reading aloud. Sure, reading aloud is integral to oral interpretation. In fact, at the level of technique alone, reading aloud *well* is an important part of oral interpretation. But when it is *only* reading aloud, it is not oral interpretation.

Acting is a performing art. Singing is a performing art. Dancing is a performing art. Oral interpretation is one of the performing arts.

Oral Interpretation Is Not Public Speaking

One of the main differences between oral interpretation and public speaking is function. A public speech is a communication event mostly focused on content. An oral interpretation performance is an artistic event focused on the aesthetic experience.

A public speaker uses words crafted specifically for that event. The oral interpreter uses words that are crafted for artistic purposes, unrestricted by the performance event. The best public speakers use an extemporaneous delivery style, work from notes, and never use the exact same words when they practice or deliver the speech. The oral interpreter not only uses the same words in every rehearsal and performance, but also makes an error if there is a deviation from those words. (It is not an Emily Dickinson poem anymore if I change the words.) A good public speaker makes eye contact with the audience as much as the circumstances allow. An oral interpretation performer may or may not make eye contact, depending on the performance choices she makes.

There are some public speaking courses that include a unit on oral interpretation. The art of oral interpretation is a good tool for helping people overcome the fear of speaking in public. Because the words are read, the neophyte public speaker feels safe knowing exactly what she will say.

There are a host of ways wherein we could compare public speaking and oral interpretation. For the purposes of this text, it is enough to know that oral interpretation is not public speaking and that the main difference, as noted above, is in the intent of the event.

Oral Interpretation Is Not Acting

Oral interpretation is not acting. Yet the oral interpretation performer and actor can use similar techniques and approaches to performance. An actor memorizes the lines, but an oral interpretation performer may or may not memorize the piece. An actor wears a costume. Oral interpretation performers generally do not wear costumes. An actor generally uses props, and most oral interpretation performers do not. An actor usually performs on a set, frequently a very elaborate set. Rarely is there a set for an oral interpretation performance. Actors, in character, speak directly to other actors. Oral interpretation performers rarely speak directly to another performer. Where is the line between acting and oral interpretation? I am not sure.

If a lone performer, dressed nicely but not wearing a costume, stands center stage before an audience and, holding a script, reads an epic poem with great eloquence, vivid expression, and vigorous gusto . . . then that is oral interpretation.

If several actors wearing costumes occupy a stage on which a set has been built, and they handle many props while they address one another in character, using lines they have memorized . . . then that is acting.

But what about Max McLean? McLean is a stage actor who memorizes large portions of the Bible. I have seen him perform alone on a stage, with a set, in costume, with lighting and sound effects. Speaking verbatim words from the Bible, McLean takes his audience through a host of emotions and provides a moving theatrical experience. Is he acting, or is it oral interpretation?

While in college, I saw a performer decked out in a seaman's coat and cap. He paced about an empty stage (actually, it was a lecture hall), and kept us spellbound for two hours as he recited large portions of *Moby Dick*. Was he acting, or was it oral interpretation?

What about Patrick Stewart's one-man production of *A Christmas Carol*? Stewart is best known as an actor. His two-hour presentation of *A*

Christmas Carol does not use a set or costumes. Dressed in formal wear he *tells* the tale himself. Charles Dickens used to *read* the tale to audiences. Stewart works from memory, and Dickens worked from a manuscript. While Stewart's performance leans toward acting, both are engaged in oral interpretation.

In the fall of 2001, I directed two productions based on the works of author Robert Fulghum. At the local high school, I directed the theatrical version of *All I Really Need to Know I Learned in Kindergarten.* We called it the spring play. The actors all memorized their lines. When it was appropriate, they addressed each other directly and in character. We had a simple set and used lighting and sound effects.

At the same time, for a community theater group, I directed *Uh-Oh, Here Comes Christmas,* also based on the works of Fulghum. We had simple costuming, a simple set, and all the performers carried their scripts for the entire performance. In this Christmas show, for the most part, all the lines were directed toward the audience.

The community theater Christmas show was an oral interpretation performance, but the high school spring play crossed over into acting.

I am not sure how important it is for us to be able to distinguish absolutely between oral interpretation and acting in every instance. It is more important that a performer knows the intent of the performance at hand ("Is this acting or oral interpretation?") so that she can prepare accordingly.

Oral interpretation is the vocal presentation of literature by a performer who uses her nonverbal abilities to enhance the meaning that an audience member may derive from that literature.

Oral Interpretation Is an Obscure Art Form

The professional oral interpreter . . . or not? Imagine an immense, awe-inspiring performance hall. The limousines line up out front, and one by one they drop off star performers clothed in tuxedos and one-of-a-kind dresses. Reporters scurry about trying to get interviews with famous stars. The evening exudes the glamour and buzz of the Oscars or Tonys. Finally, after all the opening numbers, the first two presenters come to the podium. Reading from the prompter, they announce, "The nominees for best oral interpretation of a comedic poem are . . ."

We must *imagine* that scene, because it is never going to happen. The truth is that oral interpretation is an obscure art form. No one does it full-time professionally, and the only people who make any money from it are people who teach it or write books about it. Even the performers, noted previously, who present one-person shows based on a classic work of literature are considered actors. No one is a professional oral interpreter.

I have seen or been engaged in oral interpretation in churches, schools, civic arts groups, and community theater. I once saw a reader's theater about the life of Shakespeare for which I had to buy a ticket. The performers were students at an acting academy, so I suppose they may have been "professionals," but even then, they were not professional oral interpreters.

Granted, there are oral interpretation contests, but most of these are connected to educational institutions. Schools, from elementary through college, are where most oral interpretation takes place. It is a wonderful educational tool, but there are no college majors in oral interpretation. Simply put, most oral interpretation occurs at the amateur performance level.

Chapter 2

Homework Can Be Fun

The Study of Oral Interpretation

THERE ARE FOUR REASONS TO STUDY oral interpretation. First, oral interpretation is a simple performing art. By simple I mean no special performance facilities are needed. Any space where a performer can stand in front of an audience will do. If the performer can easily be seen and heard, then there is no need for lighting or sound amplification. Granted, a play can be staged using the same simple circumstances, but oral interpretation performances occur more frequently in simple settings than do plays.

Oral interpretation is simple in that anyone can perform an oral interpretation. It helps if you can read, but that is not an absolute requisite. A small child or other nonreader could memorize a piece to perform as an oral interpretation.

After reading, the other needed skill is the ability to express yourself nonverbally. People express themselves in many nonverbal ways every day. Anyone can perform an oral interpretation, anywhere. It is that simple.

A second good reason to study and engage in oral interpretation is to build self-confidence. Most people do not like being in front of groups for the purpose of making a presentation. Performance anxiety is one of the most common fears, especially among adults. Oral interpretation helps people overcome this fear in a simple, reasonably comfortable manner.

People do not like the feeling of not knowing what they will say when they get up in front of a group. That fear is why many amateur public speakers choose a manuscript style of delivery. In a manuscript delivery, the speaker reads from a manuscript. This is not a good choice for most public speaking situations because the presenter becomes a reader instead of a speaker. Reading tends to stifle the natural expression of personality, while speaking tends to promote it. In an Oral Interpretation performance, the goal is to move far beyond mere reading to full emotional expression.

In oral interpretation, the fear of not knowing what to say next is not a problem. Except for a brief introduction, there is no "speech" to create. The words to be said, the words delivered to the audience, are in the literature performed.

Another thing people do not like about being up in front of others is the feeling that everyone is focused on them. In oral interpretation, the literature acts as a buffer zone between the performer and the audience. In most cases, the oral interpretation performer will have a manuscript of the chosen literature in a binder to read from and hold between herself and the audience. The performer may, in a sense, "hide" behind the binder and get a greater feeling of security.

In most creative arenas, the older people become, the less likely they are to feel confident that they have any ability. When I was five, I was positive I could draw anything. At fifty, I am positive that I cannot. So too, with oral interpretation: younger performers will embrace it more readily, and older performers will be hesitant. Nevertheless, because it seems less risky than giving a public speech or acting outright, oral interpretation is an excellent tool to help older students and adults gain confidence about speaking in front of groups. Some public speaking courses include an oral interpretation assignment early in the schedule just for the purpose of building confidence.

A third reason to study oral interpretation is its use as another way to engage, learn about, and study literature. What better way to delve into a poem or novel than to perform it? We all know that great literature is more than just words.

Imagine reading a poem by Emily Dickinson or a novel by Charles Dickens and feeling nothing. Literature that does not move us emotionally or spiritually never makes it to the ranks of greatness. Giving voice to the emotions that great literature stirs within us is a valid way to study literature. After all, what was Dickinson's or Dickens's intent as they wrote? Did they want their readers to study the literature or feel it? Did Whitman want his readers to analyze his poems or to have their hearts and minds touched by the glory of the ideas in his words?

The final purpose for studying oral interpretation is the acquisition of a truly useful performance skill. Whether you are an individual or the director of a group, an oral interpretation performance can be rehearsed and presented quickly for a wide variety of functions.

The chair of a local fine arts group asked me to do something "dramatic" for an evening showcase of talent at a fundraiser. Knowing I could put together an oral interpretation piece in an hour or so of rehearsal, I readily agreed to participate. Since it was nearing Christmas, I found a humorous, modernized version of *The Night Before Christmas*, rehearsed it half a dozen times in two separate rehearsal periods, and performed it to the delight of all who attended. If I had needed to memorize and act out the piece, then I never would have agreed to perform. It would have taken too much time and not been worth the effort involved.

I was the artistic director for a summer theater group, and a few years back we decided we should do a Christmas show to go along with the local holiday festivities. The only reason I gave the project my blessing was because I knew we could do an hour-long reader's theater in about eight or ten hours of rehearsals. The cast and I could work it into our busy Christmas schedules. We did, and it worked wonderfully.

When someone needs help putting together some simple entertainment for a community event, a person with oral interpretation skills can provide that help. For example, if a church, synagogue, mosque, or temple needs someone to read the Holy Word during services, a person skilled in oral interpretation can be the best candidate. I once had a lady tell me that the only time her child paid attention in church was when I read the Scripture. The reason, of course, is that I did not just read it. I performed it as an oral interpretation. While most people do not know it, local talent shows are also crying out for people with oral interpretation performance abilities. Usually in a talent show, the oral interpretation performers stand out because everyone else is singing, dancing, or playing a musical instrument.

The usefulness of oral interpretation as a performance skill can enhance careers, increase popularity, and be a wonderful avenue to engage others in the joy of performance. A person who develops high-quality oral interpretation skills will find ways to use them throughout her entire life.

What is the purpose of oral interpretation? For years I taught that the purposes of public speaking are to inform, to persuade, and to entertain. In the theater criticism and history classes I completed as a student, I was taught that the purposes of theater are to educate and to entertain. It follows that the purpose of oral interpretation is also to educate (inform and persuade) and to entertain. But there is a deeper purpose that is less connected to the perfunctory functions of art. Before we get to that other purpose it is necessary to understand that oral interpretation is an expression of two artists.

Oral Interpretation Is an Expression of Two Artists

Oral interpretation is an expression of the author of the literature. Why do writers write? The answer goes beyond the pragmatic "to inform, persuade, or entertain." What is it that makes a writer want to put pen to paper or fingers to keyboard?

I have known several poets, a handful of novelists, a couple of playwrights, and even a few nonfiction writers—specifically, journalists. And I love to read about writers and the joys and struggles of writing. There is a spark of creation in writers, as in all artists. Writers have the same urge to create that all artists have, only they create with language. Writers want to put words together in ways that challenge minds, move hearts, and stir souls. Writers want to create significant meaning in the lives of readers.

The Meaning of Meaning

In classic communication theory, we teach that words do not have meaning in and of themselves. Words are only symbols, and the *meanings* attached to words only exist in the people who send and receive those symbols, not in the symbols themselves. Let me illustrate.

What does "schanchee" mean? It does not mean anything to most people. But when I say "schanchee," meaning occurs in me and in members of my family. The word was created by my daughter Julie-Rose when she was three years old. We lived near the edge of town and occasionally crows would hang out in our front yard. One day she wanted to go out to play, but the crows were there. These crows were big and vocal, so my daughter was afraid of them, but not too afraid to yell at them through the screen door. "Go away, you schanchee birds!" was her cry. I inquired as to what "schanchee" meant. She could not tell me but said, "Just look at those birds; they're schanchee." Julie-Rose knew she wanted those birds to leave, but she did not have a word to express that need. So she created one. She gave verbal expression to her inner meaning. Thus, in our house "schanchee" came to mean anything that was in an unwanted location. It is a great word, with many uses. "Dad, this spinach is schanchee." "Get your schanchee butt up to bed." "I got a schanchee grade on my test." The word itself means nothing: the meaning occurs in the people involved.

I read author Leon Uris's *Trinity* over one long weekend. The novel had enough impact on me that several times over the course of the three days I exclaimed aloud to my empty house, "Oh my gosh!" or "Whoa!" or a word or two that I would rather not put in print. Via words, Uris was able to create enough meaning in me to produce instant emotional responses.

If I choose to use a passage from *Trinity* for an oral interpretation performance, then I have a responsibility to honor Uris's effort. I have a responsibility to recognize that I am not the only artist in this oral interpretation endeavor.

Some may argue that the performer does not have a responsibility to the author, and that the performer can do whatever she wants with the work. I have read accounts of theater artists who take a work of Shakespeare and try to transmogrify it into something else. One account of a production of *Measure for Measure* managed to incorporate a television preacher and Hitler into the script. I say, why bother? If I take a passage from *Trinity* or a play by Shakespeare and perform them with so many changes as to make them unrecognizable, then what is the point? (Deconstructionist theories of art come into play here, but those theories are passé, so I will let the reader pursue them on her own.)

The very reason I would want to perform Uris or Shakespeare is *because of the meaning they create.* So whatever I do, however I perform, part of my intent is to honor the author of the work by honoring the work itself. This point can be made personal at an emotional level by way of the following exercise.

> Have each student write about something that has personal significance to her. It may be in the form of a poem, essay, letter to a significant other, or whatever that student wants it to be. Each person should "risk" a little in what is written, remembering that what she writes will be shared with the class. The finished piece should be no more than one page long and be word-processed so no one is identifiable by handwriting. The course instructor should also participate. (When I do this exercise, I usually write about a dream/goal I have for my life.) Collect all the papers and shuffle them, then pass them out randomly. Pause for ten minutes and let participants read over their pieces, or even go off and practice them, as space and time allow. Gather again and perform the pieces for one another. After everyone has performed, it is fun to try to guess who wrote what, but the key thing is to discuss how individuals *felt* as their piece was being read.

Once I had a student write about being the victim of sexual abuse and the suicide attempts that followed. It was heart-wrenching as this student exposed her much broken heart to the whole class. Her work drove home the point about trying to honor the author's intent and meaning.

All writers share some part of who they are with their readers. When literature is performed for an audience, the performer owes the author every effort to honor the author's intent, to care for the author's exposed heart.

Performer as Artist

Along with the author, there is another artist involved in an oral interpretation performance . . . you. One of the purposes of oral interpretation is for the performer to express herself as an artist. Most performers think of themselves as artists or at least recognize that they have an artistic side to their being. Some who read these words may not think of themselves as artists, or they may believe that they are not creative at all. Everyone is creative to some degree.

Consider the zeitgeist moment. A zeitgeist moment is an "ah-ha" moment when the world seems to stand still while a person's head and heart come to an incredible realization of some truth. It could be as simple as having a test handed back with an A on it when a poor grade was expected. It could be as simple as examining a clover blossom while prone in the grass on a warm spring day or as complex as coming to grips with your own death. All of us have moments when life is "realized" in some intense way. Those are *artistic* moments. Furthermore, a person's attempts to convey what was experienced in a zeitgeist moment are artistic endeavors. It makes all of us artists, at least potentially.

Along with the intent of the author, the oral interpretation performer shares her own meaning with the audience, the meaning she gets out of the literature. Every reader creates connotative meaning in herself as she reads literature. When the reader becomes a performer and tries to share the author's meaning, she shares her own meaning, as well. Part of the reason to perform an oral interpretation is to share your individual meaning with the audience.

When my daughters were small, I read to them constantly. As they grew older, we moved from picture books to chapter books. I chose books I enjoyed myself, and so one of the first chapter books they listened to was *The Lion, the Witch, and the Wardrobe* by Christian author and apologist C. S. Lewis. In the story, the lion Aslan sacrifices himself to save the life of a child who turned traitor. The witch and her cohorts put Aslan to death in a humiliating and torturous manner. As I read about Aslan's death, my youngest daughter Julie-Rose, climbed down from my lap and began to play around the room. I mistakenly assumed she lost interest in the story, and I continued to read to my older daughter, Mandi. The story takes a glorious turn when the characters discover that Aslan has come back from the dead. Lewis does a wonderful job describing the children's delight at Aslan's return and the playful romp that follows. As I read about the resurrection of Aslan, Julie-Rose began to squeal with delight and dance around the room. She had not lost interest in the story, but hearing about Aslan's death was too hard to face, and his resurrection brought back her joy. Her response to the story was a wonderful experience to behold. Even now, dozens of years later, a bright tear comes to the corner of my eye as I write about it. So naturally, when I look for a passage of prose fiction to perform for my class as an example, I choose that part of *The Lion, the Witch, and the Wardrobe*. And every time I perform it, I try to bring back at least a hint of Julie-Rose's joy. for there are two artists involved: C. S. Lewis and me.

Mind, Heart, and Spirit

There are two processes going on in the receiver of any communication: a cognitive/logical process and an affective/emotional process. How those processes work in the thoughts and feelings of the audience are worth considering in our study of oral interpretation.

An oral interpretation performance engages the audience's mind. This is the cognitive part of the process. The audience member receives the words, the symbols, sent from the performer. As noted above, the words in and of themselves do not have meaning, but the audience member decodes those words by assigning meaning to them. Initially, those words are assigned a denotative meaning. Denotative meanings are those meanings that are found in the dictionary, those meanings that are common to most people. For example, when a person reads the word "cat," she has a general idea about what a cat is. That general idea, that definition that could apply to any cat, is the denotative definition. Those denotative meanings lay the foundation of shared understanding between the author, performer, and audience. The cognitive process and the resulting shared meaning are the *bare minimum* of what should happen in a good oral interpretation performance.

Beyond that cognitive process, we encounter the affective process, the emotional process. Life would be dull, boring, and nearly meaningless if there were no emotions. If all we were was the cognitive process, and none of us had any emotions, who would care about anything? We would not be sad, but we would not be happy either. If we lived without emotions, then we would not do any performing, oral interpretation, or otherwise. We would not do any kind of art if we did not have emotions.

In a good oral interpretation performance, the audience's emotions are stirred. They feel happy, sad, angry, joyous, or awestruck. The point is that the performance makes them feel *something*. Just as with the cognitive process, feelings occur via the sharing of symbols (words) in an effort to create meaning.

Suppose a piece is performed about a woman who is so stressed out by all the complications in her life that she abandons her responsibilities for the day and goes out into the countryside, where she sits still in a flower-filled meadow hoping a butterfly will land on her. At the denotative/cognitive level, the audience comprehends the reasoning and logistics of the events. Hopefully they will engage the connotative meanings of the words and have an affective experience, as well. Connotative meanings are personal meanings. My experience of a meadow filled with butterflies is different than anyone else's, so I understand the phrase "a meadow of butterflies" differently than anyone else. Truth is, when we decode symbols, we always understand them at the denotative *and* connotative levels. We cannot help but do so.

Now suppose this piece about the stressed woman and the butterflies is performed. Everyone involved—author, performer, and audience—has some kind of experience with stress, stress relief, and butterflies, etc. The audience can then vicariously "live" the experience of the stressed woman and the butterflies, and so the performance touches them emotionally. To help the performance work for the audience, the performer adds to the words read. To the verbal speaking of the words, the performer adds nonverbal expression. The adding of the nonverbal aspects of communication is what performance is all about. My point here is that oral interpretation performers are trying to touch the minds and hearts of their audience.

Beyond the mind and heart, there is a third element. All people have a spiritual element in their being, and it is to this spiritual element that the truly great works of art speak. I am not an expert on comparative religions, but I know of no form of worship that does not involve some form of art.

Many artists and theologians point to, write about, and talk on this connection between art and the spiritual side of human beings. Theater director Peter Brook writes at length about what he calls the "spiritual theater."

I recall the words of my graduate professor Dr. Philip Walker. We gathered around him after a dress rehearsal of *Macbeth*. Armor-clad and broadsword in hand, I listened as he told us that theater allows man to "transcend himself!" I confess I am not sure what he meant, but I am sure it had to do with the spiritual.

One of the reasons there is a spiritual element to all people is humankind's search for meaning. It is possible to make a strong inductive argument that humankind as a whole and people as individuals want to know the meaning of life. We want to know what being human is all about and why.

There are at least two ways in which we as humans understand meaning. There is the meaning we give our lives. My wife and children are extremely significant to me. Their lives mean a lot to me. But that meaning is temporary. When we are all dead, that meaning ceases to exist. The *meaning that we give ourselves* is locked into time and into the limits of our own existence. If that is all I believe about meaning, then "spiritual" is not any different from "emotional." In this worldview, my emotions attach me to others and make their lives meaningful to me. But if I believe that is all there is, that it does not exist beyond my life, then there is no eternal spiritual reality.

Some will argue that there is no meaning to life, that meaning is an illusion. They will argue that, at its best, meaning in life is only what we mean to one another; it is a temporary illusion. While some say there is no meaning to life, I have yet to discover anyone who *lives* as if there is no meaning to life.

Religion, philosophy, my own experience, and the experiences of people in general suggest that there is *meaning beyond our own limits*, that the significance of being human goes beyond the limits of time and space. In my Human Communications course, I start the interpersonal unit with the assumptions on which the unit's content is based. One of those assumptions is that human beings have infinite intrinsic worth—"infinite," meaning it exists beyond the limits of time and space, and "intrinsic," meaning it is basic to the nature of what it means to be human. Intrinsic worth is worth that cannot be given or taken away. To suggest that humans have intrinsic worth is also to suggest that there is some kind of greater intelligence, greater power, an uncreated giver-of-meaning alive in the cosmos.

The belief that life has meaning suggests something about a person's worldview. If a person believes that meaning is confined to the here and now, is relative, abstract, and finite, then that person's belief suggests there is no spiritual element to life. If a person believes that meaning lives beyond here and now, has absolute aspects about it, is concrete, and is infinite, then that person's belief suggests there *is* a spiritual element to life. There is a spectrum of belief about meaning and spiritual reality that runs between the two extremes noted above.

So what is the point? Why have I digressed so far from the purpose of oral interpretation? It is because art (including the performing arts, including oral interpretation) has the ability, the potential, to touch our lives in truly significant ways—ways that touch at the core of who we are, ways that help us understand our meaning, our place in the cosmos. I do not intend to make this phenomenon sound like a somber, solemn activity. My life is touched, changed, vitalized by a moment of laughter or a flash of tears. A quirky oral interpretation performance filled with puns, non sequiturs, oxymorons, and onomatopoeia connects to my life and its meaning just as well as a piece about the search for truth in the face of death.

Let me take one more run at this attempt to explain my perspective about the relation between meaning, art, and spirituality. Belief in meaning suggests something about the human condition. If there is a spiritual reality and infinite meaning, then an individual's value and worth as a human being is significant beyond that individual's ability to understand it. If there is no spiritual reality, then an individual's value and worth as a human being is a puff of smoke soon dissipated. Oral interpretation, by engaging the mind and the heart in an exploration of meaning, engages the spirit as well.

Chapter 3

See a "New You" in the Mirror

Becoming a Performer

REGARDLESS OF THE PURPOSE OF art or the meaning engendered in the performer or her audience, the oral interpretation performer has responsibilities as a performing artist. The oral interpretation performer has a responsibility to herself, the author of the piece, and the audience.

As noted previously, authors generally risk exposing something of themselves in their writing. Students who have engaged in the writing/reading exercise in Chapter 2 will have an inkling about the meaning of that risk. The performer's responsibility to the author of the work is to recognize the writing as a piece of the author's heart/soul/being and honor it as such. By "honor" I mean to respect the work the author did. The performer should do her best to present that work in a worthy, artistic manner.

To honor the work of the author, you must strive for a technically and aesthetically high-quality performance. Technical quality means each audience member can hear and understand, at the cognitive level, every word. Aesthetic quality would mean the performer genuinely tries to touch the audience's emotions and spirit.

Technical Quality

Technical quality comes from clear articulation, appropriate pronunciation, adequate volume, and knowing the piece well enough not to stumble in the presentation. We have all heard audience members say, "I couldn't hear them," when in actuality the performer was loud enough. Usually what the audience member means is that she could not understand the words the performer was saying. I have worked with many performers I could hear just fine but could only understand about half the words they were saying because their articulation was so poor.

Articulation is the clarity of the sounds made to create spoken words. Each syllable should be clearly spoken as the author intended it. Suppose the line is written, "Did you do that?" If "D'ya do tha?" is spoken instead, then the performer has articulated poorly. Specifically, the performer left sounds out that the author intended to be included. Or suppose the performer says, "Did-da you-ah do-wah that-ah." Then the phrase has been articulated poorly by adding sounds. A performer can add or subtract sounds as a performance choice, but if the spoken words are so mangled that the audience cannot understand the words, then poor articulation choices have hurt, or even killed, the performance.

A lot of the articulation problems encountered by performers, especially neophyte performers, occur because they do not think about articulation as a choice. In our daily conversations we do not consciously think about making speech sounds clearly. We ramble along, and only think about clarity when we must repeat ourselves to make someone else understand us. In performing, clear articulation is a conscious choice. By an act of will, a performer chooses to form each spoken syllable clearly.

One simple exercise to help create clear articulation is to number syllables in a line, and then read the line slowly, making sure the requisite number of syllables are spoken. Suppose the line is, "The abominable snowman ate the hapless skier without a second thought." "The" has one syllable, "abominable" has five syllables, and so on for a total of twenty syllables in the line. Read the line and be sure to "hit" all twenty syllables. Read it like this: "The a-bom-in-a-ble snow-man ate the hap-less . . ."

It may take three or four times as long to read a piece in this manner, but it will put you on the road to clear articulation. Of course, in performance you would never speak so slowly (unless it was an artistic choice), but part of the rehearsal process is to create excellent articulation.

Clear articulation has useful applications in real life. I have never felt so embarrassed as the time I realized I was mumbling in a job interview. I was stunned when the interviewer asked me to repeat myself, and it was not because she was not listening, it was because I was not speaking clearly.

One way to improve articulation in general is to practice tongue twisters. It is helpful to speak the following lines as a class exercise so that each student can give and receive feedback about clarity. Speaking them alone is helpful, as well, but concentrate on clear articulation.

Alan the arrogant aardvark advanced on the awkward,
artificial aviators.

Bubba belched bad breath on beautiful Bertha's blooms.

Capricious Carrie couldn't call calmly; claiming calamity caused her concentric concerns.

Devious Deborah dived into the decadently delicious devil's food.

Egbert's effortless expenditure of energy exacerbated everyone's envy.

Fearful Fred's fruitless failure figured furtively in future figments.

Gregarious Greg gladly grew a garish green garnish garden.

Hapless Hanna's heartfelt hope was to hold hairy Harold's heavy hand.

Ignatius illicitly eyeballed Ignat's illegal immersion.

Jocular Jack joked joyously about jilted Jill's jerk.

Kelly's kindness keeps karate Kevin's karma keen.

Lance lamented loudly, lauding lascivious Lisa's licentious life.

Mirthful marimbas magically make melodious music.

Nice Nita's neighbor noticed Nita nearly never nagged, knowing Narnia was nearby.

Otto ousted Oola's octopus, obviously objecting to overt octagonal orifices.

Penelope's penchant for pernicious parrots perplexed Peter, who preferred petite paragons.

Queen Que's quick quackery questioned quadratic quotients querulously.

Reginald's regal regalia reeked rigorously of rigid, rancid, radical raccoons.

Smart Smeed smelled silly Sally's smile, slightly slipping south.

Turbulent, torrid Terry talked tentatively to timid Tina, taking tenacious time.

Ubiquitous Ursula urgently urged unbelievable umbrellas under uprooted urns.

Vibrant Vern verbalized vicious verbs, verbosely voicing virulent victory.

Walter's wafers wantonly withheld wacky whiffs of whimsical wags.

Xanthic Xena xylographed xenomorphic xenoliths.

Yelling "Yahoo," Yoda yielded yardage, yet yodeled Yeats's yore.

Zealous zebras zipped and zigzagged zestfully through Zetland.

One classic articulation exercise is to say the words "toy boat" ten times quickly. Try it and see what happens. Repeatedly say "toy boat" faster. Most people find themselves losing control of their tongue by the fifth or sixth repetition.

Pronunciation is also part of the performer's technical arsenal. While articulation is the *correct* formation of speech sounds, pronunciation is the *choice* of speech sound to make. How is the capital of Louisiana pronounced? Is it three syllables, as in "New Or-leans," or is it four syllables as in "New Or-le-Ans?" (Actually, the correct pronunciation of the capital of Louisiana is "Ba-ton Rouge.")

Just as each word has denotative and connotative meanings, there is also the dictionary's prescribed, right way to pronounce a word, and there is the way the author intends the word to be pronounced. In most cases the author intends the dictionary pronunciation, but there are instances, especially in character dialogue, when the author may intend an incorrect pronunciation. If an author writes the line "Y'all c'mere." it would be a mistake to perform it by saying "You all come here."

When in doubt about how to pronounce a word, and the author does not give any indication that she wants something other than the pronunciation prescribed by the dictionary, then the dictionary is the guide. For example, what is the correct pronunciation of "Arab?" Is it "air-rub" or "ay-rabb?" An incorrect pronunciation, in this instance, could easily offend someone in the audience! How about "genuine?" Is it "gen-u-eyen" or "gen-u-one?" It was not until I came back to the Midwest that I realized some people say "beu-tee-ful" instead of "beu-ti-ful" for "beautiful." So when in doubt check the dictionary.

The exception to checking the dictionary is when pronouncing proper names, especially names of places. Is the "s" on the end of "Illinois" pronounced or not? Does "Missouri" end with and "ee" sound or an "uh" sound? In these cases, wisdom lies in following the lead of the audience. How do they pronounce the word in question? When I first moved to

Illinois, it took me a while to realize that most people in Illinois do not say the "s" sound at the end. They say "Illinoi." When you are in doubt about how the audience might pronounce a word, there is always one channel of information you can access. Someone had to arrange your performance for this audience. The person who did is your contact/connection with the audience and will have a good idea about local pronunciations.

Volume is yet another technical aspect of performance. A performer will make many aesthetically related choices about volume. Regardless of how much the volume is varied for artistic effect, the one thing the performer cannot do is become so soft that the audience cannot hear. The audience must be able to hear before they can understand.

Many situations will call for electronic amplification. Usually, the host of the performance event will know the situation well enough to provide sound equipment and a person to run it. Occasionally, a performer will run into a situation where sound amplification is needed but has not been provided. If the situation allows for the requesting of amplification, then the request should be made. Another possibility is to ask the audience to move closer to the performance space, especially if they are scattered throughout a large auditorium. Sometimes in a bad situation the performer must simply do the best she can and keep even her soft moments at a respectable volume. The main thing to know about volume is that the audience must be able to hear before they can understand the spoken words.

Many times, I have heard an amateur actor misspeak a line, then go back and fix it. This kind of stumble takes quality away from the performance. The same is true in oral interpretation: a verbal stumble hurts a performance. There are two things that help prevent verbal stumbling. The first is to work from a manuscript that lends itself to easy performance. The second, and more important, is for the performer to know the piece well enough that she does not get lost. That kind of knowing is achieved through a carefully planned and well-executed rehearsal process. What is important to take note of now is that the performer who vocally stumbles as she performs, because she has not rehearsed well enough, is not honoring the work, or the author, or herself.

Making More of the Words

Part of the performer's goal is to create "more meaning" for the performed piece than words alone can make. The performer becomes a collaborator with the author of the piece when she makes choices about the nonverbal aspects of communication she will add to the words as she performs. That is what a performer does. She adds nonverbal communication to the words the author wrote. By adding the nonverbal aspects of communication, the performer touches the emotions of the audience in ways the words alone cannot. Surely the author did not intend the piece to have no effect on the reader/audience. When the performer adds nonverbal communication to the words, the performer is engaged in the interpretation of the piece.

As the performer becomes a collaborator with the author by adding her interpretation to the work, she should further honor the author by not intentionally perverting the author's intentions. I do not mean to imply that there is only one correct interpretation, one correct way to perform a piece. Nothing could be further from the truth. Anyone who has taken a good poetry class knows there are as many ways to interpret the meaning of a poem as there are people. But there are limits to what the author of any piece of literature intends it to mean. Take the *Song of Solomon*, for example. There are some verses in it that are the lover's celebration of the virtues of his beloved. Some of the imagery is archaic and could lend itself to a very sarcastic, mean-spirited interpretation ("Your hair is like a flock of goats" in Song. 4:1, NIV). Not by any stretch of the imagination could you say that sarcastic ridicule was Solomon's intent. This aspect of interpretation becomes a matter of honesty, honor, and the personal integrity of the performer. The performer should seek to convey meaning that clearly falls within the intent of the author.

Think of it this way: When the performer selects a piece to perform, it is as if the author opens his heart to the performer and offers her a piece of his soul. When the performer selects a piece, she should treat it as if the person she loves most in the world has told her a deeply intimate secret and then asked her to share it with the world. How do you share someone's heart with the world? How do you hold your greatest love's soul up for the entire world to see? You do it carefully and honorably. *Aesthetic quality* comes from the mindful selection of a piece to perform and a responsible, creative rehearsal process.

Selecting a Piece

Selecting the right piece is the first step toward a high-quality performance. The guidelines for selecting a piece to perform are mostly common sense. Selection is not a deeply mysterious process. Neverthe-less, a serious effort must be made to select a high-quality piece for an oral interpretation performance.

Audience

The first thing to consider in the selection process is the *audience*. What is known about them? Are they old, men, women, or families? What kind of educations do they have? What kind of occupations do they hold? Is there something that brings them together as an audience, such as a club meeting or church service, or will they randomly come to see this performance like the audience for a play or film? How diverse will the audience be? The more that is known about the audience, the more the performer can pick a piece appropriate for that audience. For example, performers normally would not choose a silly, funny children's story for an audience of business executives (although there are plenty of good children's stories that have a moral point applicable to the business world). Performing for the PTA? My recommendation is to avoid a pas-sage from *The Exorcist*.

Occasion

The second consideration in selecting a piece to perform is the *oc-casion* of the performance. What is the setting? Is the performance in a theater, an auditorium, a classroom, or someone's living room? Is this oral interpretation the only entertainment or one performance among many? What time of day is the performance? Did your audience just have a meal, or are you performing just before a meal is served, or during a meal? Is the audience at tables, in rows, or in a circle? Do you need amplification? Does the host provide the amplification equipment? Is this a political rally, a church service, a Boy Scout meeting, a retirement home? Is this perfor-mance solely for entertainment, or is there a theme that the performance is supposed to accentuate? How long does this performance last?

The more a performer knows about the audience and the occasion, the easier it will be to start the process toward a successful performance. There is always at least one channel of information about the audience and the occasion. Someone contacted you to arrange the performance. That contact person is either a source of information about the audi-ence and the occasion, or she knows someone who is a source. If you are performing for a specific group rather than a random audience, then find out what kinds of things the group has responded well to in the past. Find out what kinds of entertainments they have had on previous occasions. Is this performance the audience's first exposure to the art of oral interpretation? If so, you have the privilege of providing them with a great first experience.

If the performance is for a class assignment, then you want to be sure to fulfill the parameters of the assignment. If the assignment is to perform four to six minutes of short poems all written by the same author, then that is what you should do. It seems silly for me to explain this obvious aspect of the selection process, but I have been amazed over the years at those who seemed to ignore the assignment requirements to the detriment of their grade. Frequently the time limits are ignored. More than once I stopped a student ten minutes into a four-to-six-minute piece because we had to get through several more performances that day. Trust me, if the assignment is supposed to be three to five minutes long, your teacher would much rather have three minutes of a well-rehearsed polished performance than ten minutes of sloppy, impromptu reading.

Also, the student must understand the genre requirements. It hardly seems likely that a college student would confuse poetry with prose fiction, but that has happened in my classroom. Once a student who thought that reading the "Letters" section out of a popular clothing catalogue would qualify for the genre of drama. So student performers should be sure they understand the requirements of the performance assignments and diligently seek to fulfill them.

The performer's choice of material should also reflect her purpose for that performance. One purpose for every performance is entertainment. By "entertainment" I do not mean that the performance must be funny or lightweight in terms of its significance. We are entertained by things that keep our interest. Heavy-duty drama is entertainment, as is light comedy and everything in between. Beyond the purpose of entertainment, the performer may have another purpose she is trying to fulfill. Suppose an English professor invites you to class to perform the works of a specific author as an introduction to that author for the class. Or maybe you will perform the interpretation to introduce a topic for a discussion or lecture. Or maybe the performance is part of an evening that has a theme, like "love" or "Christmas" or "things that are purple." Whatever the case, you will want to pick a selection that both entertains and works for whatever other purposes are appropriate.

Appropriateness

The material the performer chooses should also be *appropriate* to her abilities as a performer. This consideration means you need a reasonably high degree of self-awareness. If you have trouble performing rhymed pieces, as I do, then you want to avoid rhymed poetry. Maybe you have trouble creating distinct character voices in dialogues. In that case, you should stay away from drama and only do prose fiction passages that do not have a lot of direct dialogue in them. If it is a highly emotional piece, the performer must know whether she can maintain the performance, even if her emotions start to run away with her. If the performer has recently experienced the death of a loved one, then a piece about death may not be the best choice. The selection process goes on into the early stages of rehearsal. After the performer has rehearsed the piece a couple of times, she will have a good idea whether it is a good match with her performance abilities.

Quality

I do not let my students perform work that is published only on the Internet. This is one step in pushing them toward performing *high-quality literature*. That is not to say that every performance must come from the ranks of the literary elite, but the quality of the literature is another important factor in the selection process. Consider your abilities, the audience, and the occasion, then find the highest-quality literature that works within that combination of variables.

As in any other art form, the parameters of what makes up good or bad literature are much debated. I am not the person to claim definitive answers in the arena of the written word, but I can summarize what literature professionals would tell you as you seek high-quality literature. Keep in mind that the following tenets are generalities. Nothing gets carved in stone.

- High-quality literature stands up to the test of time. We are still reading Shakespeare and Cervantes and Arthur Miller and Langston Hughes because their literature is timeless. *High-quality literature leaves fresh fingerprints on the souls of each new generation.* We read and perform *Romeo and Juliet* because the theme has remained true to human experience throughout the ages, and the incredible splendor of the language that is used to tell the tale still boggles our minds and prods our hearts.

- Another test of quality in literature is what the critics have to say. If the literature professionals think it is good, then who are we to argue? Of course, it is just their opinion, but if all the critics are saying it is good, then it probably is, and if they are all saying it is bad, then that most likely is true. It is not hard to find reviews of contemporary literature on the Internet. If nothing else, the student performer can ask a literature professor about the selection. Of course, the critics do not know everything. I can name several recent works for which the professionals of the literature world did not have much use but that were wildly popular with the reading public. Receiving popular acclaim does not make a work of literature high quality any more than having a large following makes professional wrestling a legitimate sport. But it is worth considering whether people, in general, enjoy the piece the performer has chosen. If the critics like it and the people like it, that is a good start.

- Look for literature that uses language well. One thing all great writers have in common is their ability to use language in ways that make common thoughts seem fresh and new. Great writers can create sentences that are much more than grammatically correct but are wonderful, as well. Of course, there are many exceptions to grammatically correct sentences in creative writing. Poetry abounds in poor syntax, and many characters in novels speak grammatically incorrect dialogue. My point is that great writers use language that makes us sit up and take notice. A great writer can describe the action of opening a door on a sun-filled day in a way that causes the reader to see that action through new eyes. In the selection process, look for a piece that uses words in ways that make you say, "Wow, that is amazing!"

- Finally, performers should consider the depth of meaning, the significance to life, of the piece they are choosing. Is the piece dealing with surface issues of life, the lightweight stuff, or is it getting into the meat of life, the weighty matters that give life its significance? I am not suggesting that you should only choose literature about love and death and justice. I remember a humorous piece about two guys fishing that was performed by a lady in one of my classes. The piece was from an outdoor sporting magazine and was filled with typical good-ole-boy-redneck humor. In terms of content, it did not deal with the weighty issues of life, but it was hysterical. We laughed so hard I had to grant her extra time without penalty because she had to pause several times while we laughed and laughed and laughed. We generally do not think of that kind of experience as a weighty matter in life, but hysterical joy is a significant part of our existence. To be metaphorical, you should think about how deeply the selection will plumb the depths of our souls, regardless of whether it is through laughter, tears, or some other emotion.

Time Limit

Once the performer has found a piece that is appropriate for the audience and the occasion, is congruent with her performance abilities, and is good literature, she has one more consideration: *time limit*. If the circumstances dictate a time limit the performer will certainly want to seek to stay within those limits. Oral interpretation performances, as part of a class, almost always have time limitations set by the instructor. In other performance situations, the time limit is set by those hosting the event, especially if there are several featured performers. Even in those circumstances when no time limit is specified, the performer will want to impose her own. When no time limit is dictated, the performer must think about the audience and the situation, then estimate a time limit for the performance.

I live in a small community. Our local Fine Arts Council hosts a Christmas program of performing arts every year. Most of the performances are musical: vocalists and instrumentalists. I once got called on to bring something "dramatic" to the evening. I was given a time limit of "about ten minutes." I knew that the audience would be families, and those families would mostly represent those in my community who are truly interested in the performing arts—in other words, the local intellectuals. We are a college town, so there are lots of intellectuals, and they are a fun group of people, true lovers of life. I began my search for a piece by immediately throwing out all the obvious choices. No *'Twas the Night Before Christmas*, no *Gift of the Magi*, no Bible passages about the birth of Jesus, no passages from *A Christmas Carol*. I wanted a piece that was fresh and fun, something that would take the audience by surprise. On hand I had a book called *A Wish for Wings that Worked* by Berkeley Breathed. It is a picture book, but the story works reasonably well without the pictures. Usually, however, I perform it for my wife's kindergarten class every year. I wanted a fresh challenge for this fine arts event. About ten days before the event, I found a book titled *Politically*

Correct Christmas Stories. One title in the book was *Frosty, the Person of Snow.* Given who the audience was, I knew that most of them would get the puns and innuendos in the politically correct version of *The Night Before Christmas,* so that is what I chose. I rehearsed it at least twice a day for nine days, and the performance went well. I was the only untraditional moment in the whole evening, which I thought was kind of refreshing.

Exercises in Piece Selection

Given the following descriptions of audiences and occasions, select a piece for each hypothetical situation. Bring the selections to class and compare and discuss the relative virtues of the different selections. My intention is for this exercise to be engaged by the whole class as an assignment. It can also work well as a personal exercise.

- The Nursing Home. A civic or church group is asked to bring an evening of entertainment out to the local nursing home. The performance will be in the recreation room, a large open space with lots of easy chairs and couches. Many of the audience members will be in wheelchairs. The audience will number between 35 and 50 people and most of the people in the audience are in their late 70s. The leader of this civic or church group asks each performer to bring five to ten minutes of entertainment as part of the evening. The performance will be on a Tuesday in the last week of March.

- Women's Issues Awareness Week. A sorority on campus is sponsoring a week of events (speakers, discussions, etc.) on "Women's Issues in the New Millennium." Toward the end of the week, they are hosting an open mic event in the student union. The setting will be similar to a coffeehouse, and the audience will be mostly college students and faculty. One of the event coordinators asks you to prepare a "short" piece to kick off the open mic event.

- Memorial Day Event. A church, temple, mosque, or synagogue is hosting the local Memorial Day commemorative event. It will take place at noon, outside on the steps of the courthouse. The audience will be a lot of retired veterans and many local businesspeople on their lunch break. Most of the communities' religious leaders will be there as well. A public address system will be provided. The weather forecast says sunshine and wind. The event coordinator asks you to bring five minutes of something that will "honor the fallen." Your five minutes will come right after a hymn, and right before a short sermon.

- The Cat Lady Goes Corporate. The community cat lady decides that living with every abandoned cat that comes along is not all that fun. She is trying to raise funds to start a legitimate animal shelter. As a kickoff fundraiser she is hosting a talent show in the local civic auditorium. This occurs in a town of about 6,000 people. She asks you to be one of the acts in the talent show.

The Performer Has a Responsibility to Know the Piece

Because I teach performing arts, time and time again I see oral interpretation performances that are slapdash, haphazard, raggedy, shabby, inferior, shoddy, pathetic, careless, common, cheap, mediocre, banal, hackneyed, ordinary, insipid, vapid, fatuous, dull, boring, empty, insincere, hollow, sterile, barren, deficient, lacking, wanting, and every other kind of bad possible. Take a guess as to the person on whom those poor performances reflected most negatively? It was not the author. It was not the audience. It was the sound technician who did such a bad job setting up the sound equipment. No, of course not! It was the performer.

Bad performances reflect most negatively on you, the performer. Each performer has a personal responsibility to perform to the best of her ability. Each performer has a responsibility to do everything she can possibly think of to make the performance an excellent experience for the audience and for herself.

First, at the *cognitive* level, the performer should know what she thinks about the piece. Logically speaking, the piece chosen must have the potential for doing well in the performance situation at hand. The length must be right and the genre acceptable. I covered most of this in the earlier section on "Selecting a Piece."

At the cognitive level, does the performer know what all the words mean denotatively? More than once I have had students stumble over some big word in a performance only to discover later that besides not being able to pronounce it, they did not even know what the word meant. When I ask them why they did not look the word up, they tell me things like, "I didn't have time," or "I didn't think it mattered," or "I don't know,

I just liked the piece." If the performer does not know the meaning of a word at the cognitive level, then how can she know the meaning of the piece with her heart?

Another cognitive way to know the piece is to understand its literary structure, its genre. If it is prose, then the performer should ask, "What makes it fit into the definition of prose?" Is it a narrative passage, a dialogue, what? If it is a poem, what makes it a poem, and does it meet the definition of one of the specific kinds of poetry (sonnet, haiku)? Does it use metaphor or simile?

What does the performer know about the author? What is the social and cultural milieu in which this piece is written? You should learn everything you can about the piece at the logical, cognitive, knowledge level.

The performer also needs to know what she feels about the piece. Can the performer articulate why she likes it? What emotions does it touch? *Emotional* knowing is not as easy to describe in words as cognitive knowing, but emotional response is the foundation for your interpretation. When the performer decodes the words the author wrote, it is the connotative meaning that stirs her soul, makes her laugh or cry. The performer should be able to explain at least some of how she feels in response to the piece she chooses to perform.

What are the *spiritual* implications of the piece? It can be useful to juxtapose the feelings the piece generates in the performer with her own thoughts and feelings about life in general. Of course, before the performer can do that, she must be in touch with her own beliefs and feelings. As an exercise, it can be useful for the performer to try to articulate what she believes about the worth of human existence and the "why" of human existence. In other words, what do you truly believe about why we are here, and what does this piece of literature have to say about that belief?

As the performer begins to rehearse the piece, she must be free to respond to her creative urges. In doing so, the performer honors herself as a creative artist. What does she want to do with the piece? What performance choices will she make to bring her interpretation of the piece to the audience? Let me urge each potential performer who is reading this to learn to be open to the creative urges that occur in the selection/rehearsal process. Openness to creative urges can be a big risk, but unless the performer risks failure, she will never have success.

While it is the performer's responsibility to treat the piece as a part of the author's heart, it is also her responsibility to treat the overall performance as a part of her own heart. Regardless of whether the performance is funny, serious, crazy, deep, or off the wall the performer should see it as sharing a part of her heart, a part of her soul with the audience. That is why it is called "art."

In many ways, your responsibility to the audience is the most important. After all, without the audience there is no performance. Performers, via their performance, are trying to connect with, touch, get into the hearts, minds, and souls of the audience. The audience gives the performer the privilege of being their center of attention. Performers should honor that gift by performing well.

Your first responsibility to the audience is to have a technically high-quality performance. As noted previously, each performer's articulation, volume, pronunciation, and familiarity with the piece should be immaculate. If the audience cannot hear words, or cannot understand the words, or if the performer breaks the flow of the performance by stumbling through the piece, then she will lose the audience. A performance that is low-quality in its technical aspects has little chance of touching the hearts and minds of the audience in any significant manner.

As performers rehearse and perform an oral interpretation, each should strive to honor the author, herself, and the audience in every way possible. Impress this image on your mind: take a piece of the author's heart, combine it with your own, and use that combination to touch the hearts of the audience.

Chapter 4

It Is Not What You Say, But How You Say It

The Vocal Aspects of
Nonverbal Communication

CONSIDER THE FOLLOWING:

Say "Ahh."

Say "Ahh" with joy.

Say "Ahh" angrily.

Say "Ahh" sadly.

Say "Ahh" as if curious, or scared, or in ecstasy, or confused, or as having a life-changing revelation.

What is the difference between all these "Ahhs?" It is the way they sound, and the way you look when you say them. They all have different variations in pitch and volume, and your facial expression and body language are different for each one. Simply put, your nonverbal expression for each "Ahh" is different.

What does a singer, actor, or oral interpretation performer do with the words the lyricist or author has provided? The performer adds the nonverbal to the verbal. In this context, think of *verbal* as the word itself, the phonetic sounds that make up the word. Think of *nonverbal* as everything else about how you say the word. All the aspects of nonverbal communication are the performer's tools for expression when she performs. In acting, singing, and oral interpretation, the performer's task is to add nonverbal to the verbal in ways that enhance the meaning of the words to the audience.

The nonverbal is an incredibly powerful part of all spoken communications. Whether you have a casual conversation with your friends or the greatest actor alive performs a Shakespearean soliloquy, it is the nonverbal that conveys most of the intended meaning. Depending on which communications expert you choose to believe, the nonverbal conveys as much as 95% to 100% of the intended meaning. I have not read any communications expert yet (and I have read a lot of them) who says that the nonverbal conveys less than 50% of the intended meaning of spoken words. Try this experiment:

> Pair up with another student and read this paragraph to each other. The reader should try to avoid any nonverbal addition to the words. This is called "rote" reading. The idea is to say each word without any vocal inflection. No changes in pitch, volume, rate, or rhythm should occur. Read the paragraph without any facial expression. Do not use gestures, movement, or body language of any kind. It is not easy to read in a completely rote manner, so the student who is listening will give feedback. When the listener thinks the reader is adding nonverbals to the words, the listener will signal the reader. The signal can be as simple as a raised hand, but my favorite is to make a buzzer sound. After both of you have read the paragraph aloud, with the other giving feedback, read the paragraph to each other again as naturally as possible. Do not try to add any nonverbals, but do not try to keep them out either.

I hope you see the incredible difference the nonverbal makes in the intended meaning.

> Now, read one more time. Each person picks an emotion to covey. Read the paragraph as if you are angry, or sad, or anxious, or bored. Do not tell your partner what emotion you are going after and see if she can guess.

The difference the nonverbal makes is clear. Do one more experiment.

> Go to the library and check out a foreign film, one in which the dialogue is not in a language you speak. If the film has subtitles, try to ignore them and watch the film for a while. How much can you tell about what is happening in the film? Probably a good deal. But a good film tells a story in pictures, so take one more experimental step. Close your eyes and just listen to the dialogue. What can you understand about the conversation? Do the moods and emotions of the speakers come through? With

your eyes still closed, imagine the facial expressions that go with the words. Open your eyes and see if the facial expressions you imagined are congruent with what is on the screen.

The point will be clear. Besides what the experts tell us about nonverbal communication, the power of nonverbal communication is evident to all.

One of the important differences between verbal and nonverbal communication is that verbal communication is a conscious activity, and nonverbal communication is an unconscious activity. When we speak, we consciously choose the words we say. It is a rapid, fluid process, and we speak sentences as we compose them, but it is still a conscious activity. Our active will is involved in making the word choices.

In normal conversations, the nonverbal that we affix to the verbal is not consciously added. When I ran into a colleague's office to announce that our theater group had received a government grant, I was not thinking, "Now I will talk in an excited, celebratory tone." But I was genuinely excited, and the excitement naturally showed in my nonverbal communication. Through our nonverbal communications we unintentionally reveal our moods and emotions. Our personality shows through our nonverbal. It is not by an act of conscious will that I speak louder when I am angry, or that my voice gets weak when I am distraught.

When we consciously choose to control the use of our nonverbal communications, it becomes a powerful communications tool. Imagine two people arguing. One is in an uncontrolled, red-faced, finger-pointing, yelling mode, and the other maintains a calm expression on her face and in her voice. In that picture, who has the upper hand? Studies suggest that by correctly controlling our nonverbal communications, we can more readily convince others to believe us and to agree with us. Such is the power of nonverbal communication.

We learn the meaning of nonverbal communication by experience, and experience suggests that our understanding of the nonverbal is instinctive. By the time a child is fluent in her native language, she has unconsciously mastered the sending and receiving of nonverbal communications. In fact, she has sent nonverbal communications from her very first wail when the doctor wrestled her from the comfort of the womb out into this crazy world. She has also received and interpreted nonverbal communications from day one. When her mom spoke to her in a cooing voice, she did not understand the words, but she understood the nonverbal, and she responded with giggles and smiles. It is as if we are all designed to understand the sending and receiving of nonverbal communications. It is intrinsic to being human.

Performing—whether it is acting, oral interpretation, or even singing—is consciously controlling the nonverbal that the performer adds to the verbal. When you perform, by an act of the will you *choose* to sound happy, or sad, or anxious, or confused, or whatever, even though you are not truly any of those things while performing. The choices you make about your nonverbal communications are preplanned and rehearsed.

Wait a minute, here! If I go watch a play, how can I be affected by the performance if I know that none of it is real? How can I feel sad for the tragic hero if I know that he is just choosing to appear sad?

I am affected because I consciously or unconsciously choose to suspend my disbelief. In theater theory, this action on the part of the audience is referred to as the "suspension of disbelief." We suspend our disbelief all the time when watching a movie or television program or play. We know the actors are pretending, but we choose to ignore that knowledge. In fact, this is easy to do, because of the power of nonverbal communications. Good actors or oral interpretation performers can control their nonverbal so well that they make it easy for the audience to suspend disbelief.

Paralanguage: If a Word Made a Sound in a Forest, Would Anyone Hear It?

The sound of a spoken word, apart from the phonetic sounds that make up the word, is called *paralanguage*. Paralanguage is the pitch, rate, volume, and rhythm of the spoken word. Remember the rote exercise earlier in which the performer speaks in a rote way and consciously tries to avoid any paralanguage? When the performer speaks in normal conversation, she naturally and unconsciously adds paralanguage, and when she performs, she *consciously* adds paralanguage. Paralanguage is the performer's most important nonverbal vocal tool.

A Note on Pitch

Pitch is the relative highness or lowness of sound. On a piano keyboard, the highest notes are at the right end and the lowest are at the left. Every word you speak has pitch. Even when the performer tries to speak in a rote manner, the words still have pitch, and the performer just tries to keep the pitch from changing word to word.

In human beings, low-pitched voices are associated with males and high-pitched voices are associated with females. This is because most men have vocal folds (another name for vocal cords) that are longer than most women's vocal cords. Because most men's vocal cords are longer than most women's vocal cords, the men's cords vibrate more slowly and so produce a lower note. There are exceptions. Some men speak naturally in a higher note than most other men, and some women speak in a lower note than most other women. When we run into these phenomena, we think it a bit odd, but there is nothing right or wrong about the pitch of a person's natural voice.

I recall seeing Soviet dissident Aleksandr Solzhenitsyn being interviewed on TV. The famous Russian novelist was a short, burly man with a barrel chest and a long dark beard. The interviewer asked the first question. Solzhenitsyn stroked his beard, thought for a moment, and spoke in a voice that sounded a lot like Mickey Mouse. It caused me a bit of cognitive dissonance, and I did not hear his first few words because of it. Not that it was wrong for him to have a high, squeaky voice, but how he looked and how he sounded were not congruent with most cultural expectations. Unfortunately, sometimes men who naturally speak in a high voice and women who naturally speak in a low voice are at a social/cultural disadvantage in the workplace and social situations. There may be an unconscious bias against them because the way they sound does not meet the stereotype for their gender.

Pitch conveys a great deal more than simply some hints about a person's gender. There were times when I was very afraid, and my voice took on a husky, low tone. There were also times when I was startled, and my shriek came out in a high note. In both instances I was scared, but my nonverbal conveyed differences about my state of fright. Try this simple experiment:

Say, "Did you do that?"

The first time you speak the phrase, choose a medium note for "Did you do" and a high note for "that?"

The second time you speak the phrase, keep the medium pitch for the first three words, and go with a low note for the last.

Partner with someone and try it out a few times. Which one sounds more like a question? Which one sounds like there is more concern on the part of the speaker? Pitch obviously changes the meaning.

In English, a change in pitch affects the connotative meaning of a word, but there are some languages in which a change in pitch changes the denotative meaning. I read about a missionary who was working with Wycliffe Bible Translators. She was learning a language that did not have any written form. It was a language that relied on pitch to change meaning as well as phonetics. When trying to help a sad friend she said, "Why are you crying?" The friend responded with a quizzical look. The missionary later realized she had said, "Why are you sewing?" In that language, the words for "crying" and "sewing" were the same except for the pitch at which they were spoken. This phenomenon could pose interesting problems for performers. How would you use pitch in performance when it can change the denotative meaning of words? I would guess that the speakers of languages that use pitch to change denotative meaning understand the connection between paralanguage and the expression of emotion in ways different than most English speakers.

Volume Speaks Volumes

Volume is a second important aspect of paralanguage. As I noted before, you must always have enough volume to be heard by the whole audience, but beyond that, changes in volume affect the connotative meaning of the word. Try this exercise:

> Say the phrase "What are you doing here?" without changing pitch
> but with changes in volume. Say it very softly, in a whisper. Then
> scream it as loud as you can without hurting your vocal folds.

The change in volume changes the meaning. The whispered phrase may be something secret that lovers say when they unexpectedly meet in public. The yelled phrase might be the parent finding the underage child in a bar. As with pitch, volume can show off a range of emotions from anger to joy, from confusion to certainty, and is a key tool for you as a performer.

Reading Rate

Ever met any one who talks really fast, and what they say sounds like this sentence looks? Rate is the speed of utterance. Rate is the number of syllables you can speak in X amount of time. The average person, speaking in everyday conversation, speaks somewhere between 100 and

150 words a minute. Just like pitch and volume, rate conveys emotion and changes the connotative meaning of words. When we are excited, we speak more quickly, and more slowly when we are in a contemplative mood. Try this:

> Without changing pitch or volume say, "I went to the store and bought a new book." Say it as fast as you can. Say it very slowly.

Changes in speed of utterance will change the feeling and the meaning of the phrase.

Rate can be varied for whole phrases or individual words. I can say "rhinoceros" quickly or slowly and change the connotative meaning of the word. When I speed up or slow down individual words, I am using a combination of rate and rhythm. We will get to rhythm in a moment but, first, a word of caution about speed. Speed tends to kill articulation.

When the performer speaks very rapidly, she will most likely lose some clarity in her articulation. This, of course, works against the performer and hurts her performance. But if the performer keeps her articulation clear, then she may speak as quickly as she wants, and the audience will be able to understand her. While we speak at 100 to 150 words a minute, we think at 400 to 1,000 words a minute. (I have no idea how researchers figured this out, but I just take their word for it.) The speed at which we send words is limited by the mechanics of speech. Our vocal folds, tongue, and lips can only move so fast. But our comprehension of the spoken word is only limited to the speed of thought. So unless the performer has some kind of superpower and can speak at an inhuman rate, if she keeps her articulation clear, she may speak as fast as she wants.

Rhythm of Life

Have you ever been speaking to someone when she put a long pause in the middle of the sentence, and you hung there waiting for her to finish? I had a friend, a brilliant theatrical designer, who had that odd habit. He would say something to me like, "Rich, I think we can decrease the weight of these platforms by using . . . one by four lumber, without hurting the . . . structural integrity." He did not stutter, and he was not struggling for the right words. He was a deep thinker and careful communicator who changed the composition of the sentences he spoke as he spoke them. He knew he did this, and we would tease him about it. It was a rhythm thing.

Rhythm is where you put the pauses in the spoken word. It is also the length of the pauses. Like all the other aspects of paralanguage, variations in rhythm affect connotative meaning. Try this:

> Say, "I don't want to go." Try to keep all variation in paralanguage out except for rhythm. Say it once with very short pauses between the words, and again with very long pauses. How does it change the meaning? Say it again and vary the length of the pauses between the words. What kind of effects can you create?

Rhythm affects the rate of a sentence in that the performer says the words quickly but puts long pauses between the words. Try this:

> Say, "Animals aren't always animated." Say the words themselves quickly but put a pause between the words. It is most useful for you to think of rate and rhythm as one aspect of paralanguage, rather than two. While they can be analyzed separately, in practical application, they always go together.

Your Voice is *Your* Voice

There is one other aspect of paralanguage that is harder to define. The overall quality of a person's voice is an aspect of paralanguage, and it does affect the intended meaning of the spoken word. Think of the gravelly-voiced Country Western singer who sounds like he gargles broken glass every day. Think of any high-profile politician, someone you have heard on television and radio a lot. Think of some of the action-hero movie star types. Can you hear the voices of these people in your head? How is it that you can recognize someone's voice over the phone? We can recognize someone's voice because, just like our faces, our voices are unique.

The unique combination of vocal folds, tongue shape, bone structure, and resonant cavities in my head give my voice a unique sound. Just as we all have fingerprints, we also have a voiceprint that can be measured and identified electronically. Impressionists learn to manipulate paralanguage to cause their voice to sound eerily like the voice of someone famous. This manipulation of general voice quality is yet another tool the performer has at her disposal.

All Together Now

When all the aspects of paralanguage are put together, as they are in any spoken communication, there are an infinite variety of combinations.

And those combinations bring an infinite spectrum of possible intended meanings to the words you say. Remember that the paralanguage the performer uses can be up to 100% of the performer's intended meaning, apart from the words. By a simple manipulation of paralanguage, the performer can *mean* the opposite of what she *says*. In other words, the denotative meaning is opposite the connotative meaning. The classic example is the person who is screaming at top volume, at the higher end of his pitch range, about how he is not mad, as in, "I am not mad! Not at all! I am not mad!"

Bottom line: In performance, as in everyday life, the way you say something is as important as what you say.

Exercises in Understanding and Using Paralanguage

There are numerous reasons to engage in paralanguage exercises. Just as with any other part of you, if you do not exercise your speaking voice, then you will not be able to do much with it. Sure, most of us speak thousands of words daily as we talk to friends and family. But in all that daily talking we do not explore what we can do with our voices in any consciously creative way. These paralanguage exercises are one way to learn what you can really do with your voice. If nothing else, they can be helpful in making you aware of the paralanguage functions of your voice.

Also, these kinds of exercises are valuable in helping the performer discover performance choices for a piece she is working on. By imposing paralanguage choices on the piece, the performer forces herself to get away from the performance choices she would naturally make. Not that her natural performance instincts would be wrong—there is no right or wrong in this arena—but compelling the performer's paralanguage into some not-so-natural choices may cause her to perceive new performance possibilities.

Remember that in all these exercises you are speaking, not singing. Give your vocal folds a real workout, but in this case ignore the "no pain, no gain" cliché. If you have pain in your vocal folds, then you have gone too far.

Creative play (as when little kids go out and "play") is a key element in all these exercises. You should have fun doing them. Also, in that same spirit, there are many variations on these exercises that I have not included. The possibilities are infinite. So make up some of your own exercises. Play!

Pitch. Remember that in all these pitch exercises you are trying to keep the same volume.

- You do not have to be a singer to exercise your voice in terms of pitch. Even if you cannot carry a tune when you sing, it is fun and useful to know the extent of the high and low notes you can reach with your spoken voice. Say "Aaaaaaah." Start saying "Aaaaaaah" in as low a note as you can, and finish saying "Aaaaaaah" at as high a note as you can. Stretch it out so you use a full breath to go from the low to the high. Then go back from the high to the low. Try to keep the volume the same throughout so you do not mistake changes in volume for changes in pitch. Experiment with how low you can go. Do the same with how high you can go. Do not rush it. Take the full breath to go between the extremes. Now change the "word" you are saying. Say "Ooo" (rhyming with "you"). Do all the same things you did with "Aaaaaaah." Now try "Oh" (rhyming with "go"). Now try "Eee" (rhyming with "me"). Now try "Aye" (rhyming with "I"). Now try "Ay" (rhyming with "hay"). Try it with whatever other syllables come to mind. Try it with a few one-syllable words.

- Pick a fun sentence. Use one of the tongue twisters from the articulation exercises or find your own. Speak the sentence varying the pitch but not the volume. Start low and go high, speaking each word at a higher note. Start high and go low. Say alternate words high, then low. Speak each word at any randomly different note than the previous word.

- Work as a group. Pick a piece and distribute a copy to everyone. Stand in a circle. Go around the circle, each of you reading one word of the piece. The first person reads her word at as low a note as possible. The second person reads her word at a slightly higher note, and so on around the circle. When you have reached the extremes of your individual ability, continue to read but go back down the scale. There are lots of variations on this exercise. Have the first person read as low as possible, the second read as high as possible, the third low again, and so on. Each person reads her word at a different note than the previous person. Do not go around the circle. One person reads the first word at the note she thinks sounds best, and when someone gets a feel for the second word, she reads it. Someone else reads the third word and so on. Try each of the above but read whole sentences instead of just words.

Volume. When you experiment with volume you want to be very careful not to hurt your vocal folds. Yelling too loud, or too long, is one simple way to damage vocal folds. If you have ever yelled your head off at a sports event and left the game with a sore throat, then you know what I mean. Do all the exercises from above in the "Pitch" section, only this time vary the volume, not the pitch.

Rate and Rhythm. I am combining the exercises for rate and the exercises for rhythm, as these paralanguage functions are basically inseparable in practice. and it is mostly for academic understanding that we have dealt with them separately up to this point.

Remember that rate and rhythm deal with how fast or slow you speak the words, and the length of the silences between the words. As you work the rate and rhythm exercises, try to stay away from variations in pitch and volume.

- Find a long, complicated sentence. Keeping your articulation as clear as possible, speak the sentence as fast as possible. Choose a partner and have a contest. Select an unbiased third party and let her judge between the two of you as to who can say the sentence faster while keeping the articulation clear.

- Using the same sentence, become a metronome. Speak each syllable separately, at a steady rate. Get a metronome. (There are smartphone apps.) Try matching its beat. Speed it up. Slow it down.

- Say the same sentence. Start slow and speed up as you speak. Start fast and slow down as you speak.

- Say "rhinoceros." See if you can use up one whole breath to speak that one word. Time it with a stopwatch. Keep your articulation clear. See how many times you can say "rhinoceros" in one breath. In one minute. Try it with other long words.

- Speak a sentence and purposefully put in unnatural pauses. Make the length of the silences between the words start out short and then lengthen them as you speak the sentence. Make the silences start out long and then shorten them as you speak the sentence.

- As a group, form into a circle, and everyone should have a copy of the same text. One person speaks the first word of the piece. She should say the word as slowly or as quickly as she wants. The second word is spoken by the second person, but only after she feels that there is an appropriate pause. Continue around the circle, with all the performers inserting pauses that are as long or as short as they want and speaking the word as quickly or slowly as they want.

Combined Pitch, Volume, Rate, and Rhythm Exercises

- Complete any of the activities noted above, but instead of varying just one element, vary two, or three, or all four.

- Have a paralanguage contest. Select some unbiased judges if that is possible and have them listen as each of you reads the same piece of literature with as much variation in all four aspects of paralanguage as possible. The winner is the person who can go to the extreme limits and also cover everything in between. Read the piece in question backwards so the words do not get in the way.

- Have a paralanguage war, free-for-all. Choose some small teams. You will all need a copy of the same piece of literature. Your teams will line up facing each other. If there are three teams, you should form a triangle, if four teams form a square. Each team should number their members one, two, three. To start the war, free-for-all, have the first member of the first team take a step toward the opposing team(s) while saying a word or phrase from the piece using as much paralanguage as she can muster. This action constitutes the first volley. The first member of the second team then sends a volley. The third does likewise, and so on. Each volley should follow the previous as quickly as possible, and each volley should be as unlike the previous, in terms of paralanguage, as possible. When members of opposing teams meet in the middle, they just step around each other, and the war, free-for-all continues until all the teams have regrouped on the other side of the playing space.

- *Environment and Paralanguage.* The object of this exercise is to take your piece of literature and work on it in as many diverse environments as possible. Most of you will probably rehearse in your dorm room or apartment. Try to break free from that and see how different environments affect your use of paralanguage. Try rehearsing your piece in the shower (probably with the water off, but I will leave that choice up to you). Bathrooms have fun acoustics (which is one of the reasons people like to sing in the shower). Turn all the lights off and rehearse your piece via flashlight. If you have access to a theater, go rehearse your piece on stage. If you can get into the classroom where you will perform the piece, try rehearsing there. Go outside and rehearse. Walk down a busy street and perform the piece as you walk. If it is a big, crowded city, then no one will even notice, or if they do notice, stop and hold out your hat. A performer is worthy of receiving whatever wages are available. Try your piece out in a garage, a basement, on a roof, in a cave, at the zoo. What kind of paralanguage do you feel inspired to add to the piece in these varying settings?

Chapter 5

The Truthful Body

The Physical Aspects of Nonverbal Communication

ANOTHER VITAL ASPECT OF NONVERBAL language is what some have called "body language," and specifically how you "look." For the purposes of this textbook, we will call this aspect of nonverbal language *visual communication*. The performer's visual communication is all that is received by the people she is communicating with (apart from what is heard). How you look to someone else and what they think that look means is visual communication. Everyone engages in visual communication all the time. The clothes you chose to wear today, the way you comb your hair and put on makeup are all part of your visual communication.

If someone comes into my office as I write these words, my posture at the computer would tell them something. Hopefully it would tell them that I am concentrating on my work. A moment ago, if someone had come into my office, she would have found me leaning back in my chair with my hands behind my head and my feet up. Even though I was still concentrating on my work, my visual communication said something different.

How you look as you perform a piece of literature has a deep impact on the meaning the audience will receive. Visual communication is part of the nonverbal language that you will consciously and unconsciously add to a piece as you perform it.

Turn on the TV, turn off the sound. Watch. What can you tell about the people and the communications they are sending to each other? Surely a great deal, and most of it has to do with their emotions and the meanings of their emotions. You can tell if the characters are pained, happy, angry, frustrated, sad, anxious, or ecstatic, all from the way they look. And in this case, actors on TV have consciously worked on the kind of

49

image they will project from moment to moment as they perform. Actors make conscious choices about the emotions they want to convey and how they will make those emotions apparent to the audience. You, as an oral interpretation performer, must do likewise. You want to choose how your face will look when you read a line, what your hands will do, what kind of body posture you will have. You want to know where you will look when you are not looking at the script and how you hope that focus will affect the audience.

Just like acting, oral interpretation is using the nonverbal together with the verbal in the hope of having an impact on the audience beyond the meaning of the words.

The Expressive Face

Think of your mother, or brother, or father, or best friend, or wife, or George Washington. See this person in your mind. What do you see? Elbow? Knees? Left foot? When you think of a particular person you usually think of her face. The face is the focal point of a person's body. Granted, some people have attractive or unusual physical attributes that we associate with them, but when we think of the identity of those people, it is the face we identify. Some communications theorists, especially those who write books about nonverbal communication, suggest that more visual communications occur via a person's face than the rest of the body in its entirety. In other words, if my body is dancing, but my face is crying, it is my face others will tend to believe. (That is why directors of amateur theater productions are always yelling "smile" at the chorus line.)

Clearly, as an oral interpretation performer, your face is a very important channel of communication. How does your face look? Can you see your face in your mind's eye? Do you know what you look like when you are happy, sad, angry, confused? Get in front of a mirror and try to look happy. How does your face feel when you look happy? Try an impatient look. How does your face look/feel when you are impatient? I recall reading a magazine article about a popular comedian who was hosting the Oscar awards. Before going on he would stand in front of a mirror and practice various expressions. You should do the same. As a performer you should be in touch with how your face looks and feels as you express various emotions. Your face is a key performance tool.

The Eyes Have It

I was walking down the street in San Francisco. I turned the corner and was suddenly in the middle of an art show. San Francisco is like that; you never know where turning a corner will take you. As I walked along the rows of paintings, I came to a section of green paintings. There were landscapes and portraits and stills. They were all wonderful, and they were all in various shades of green. As I looked at the work, the artist approached me. He appeared the classic artist, with a white smock, a Van Dyke beard, and a black beret on his head. After a few moments of conversation, he asked me to take off my sunglasses, and it was then that I noticed he was concentrating intently on my face as we talked. He reminded me of my Uncle Anton. Not the way the artist looked but the way he talked to me was like the way my Uncle Anton, who was deaf, talked to me. I asked the artist if he was reading my lips and he said he was. Even though he was reading my *lips*, he had asked me to take off my sunglasses to see what my *eyes* were saying. The eyes are capable of powerful expression.

Every once in a while, I grab my wife Carol Ann and look into her eyes to see what is there, to see what is really going on inside her. A person's eyes tend to tell the truth about that person. Not the truth about a person's character; the old adage that a person with shifty eyes is a crook is an old myth. No, eyes tell the truth about a person's emotional state. Eyes tell the truth about joy, and sorrow, and fear, and peace as they occur in the emotions.

The oral interpretation performer will make conscious and unconscious decisions about where she focuses, and the expressive power of the eyes will go with that focus. It is important to be aware of what your eyes do as you perform.

By *focus* I mean where the performer sends her gaze. Does she look at the audience? If so, does she make eye contact with them? If she is not looking at the audience, then where is she looking? Over the audience at the walls? At the ceiling? At the floor?

Remembering the expressive power of the face and eyes, the first thing you need to understand about focus is that it should not be on the script. As an oral interpretation performer, you should keep your face out of the script as much as possible. Even if the performer does not look at the audience, she wants them to see her face. If the performer is looking down at the script, then the audience is not seeing her face as well as they could. If the performer holds the script high enough that she does not have to look down, then the script itself may block the audience's view. The best choice is for the performer to know the script well enough that she does not have to look at it constantly.

The decisions the performer makes about whether to look at the audience will depend on many things. The author's intent, the mood of the piece, and the performer's intent all need to be considered.

Suppose the piece is a poem that is basically an intrapersonal reflection on life. ("Intrapersonal" means communications with oneself.) In that case, to go with the author's mood, it is best not to look at the audience. The performer may choose to perform the poem in a meditative manner, without looking at the audience, and the performance is as if the audience is eavesdropping on someone's private thoughts.

Or the performer could choose to do the same piece and look right at the audience, even making eye contact with them. Then the performance would take on a more presentational feel. ("Presentational," as a performance style, means the performer does not pretend that the audience is not there, but recognizes them and presents the performance directly to them.) In this example, neither choice of focus—looking at the audience or not—is wrong or right. It depends on what the performer wants to do with the piece, what the performer wants to try to accomplish in the hearts and minds of the audience.

Suppose the performer has a piece about someone who watches something else and describes it. Maybe it is an old man watching his grandchildren play, or a scientist watching her experiment blow up. In these cases, the performer may not want to look at the audience because it is important for the performer to try to make the audience see what the character sees. In this case, what the audience sees on the performer's face becomes crucial, and eye contact may get in the way.

When performing a dialogue between two or more characters, it is imperative that each character have her own focus. This split focus is especially important if the dialogue is from a script. When you perform a dialogue out of prose fiction, you have the advantage of signal phrases such as "Bill replied" or "Sally asked" to help the audience keep the characters straight. Dialogue from a script does not have that advantage, so the performer must do everything she can to keep the characters separated in the minds of the audience. Giving each character a different focus is key to keeping them clearly separated.

What if the performer has a dialogue with two characters, Phred and Phelicia. One of the performer's goals is to make it clear to the audience when Phred is speaking and when Phelicia is speaking. If the audience loses track of who is speaking, then the confusion created in the minds of the audience members takes away much of the potential impact of the piece. So to help keep Phred and Phelicia separate, the performer gives each of them a different focus.

Imagine you are standing squarely face to face with Phrank. Now imagine Phred standing almost shoulder to shoulder on one side of Phrank and Phelicia in the same spot on the other side of Phrank. So when you talk to Phrank you are looking straight ahead, when you talk to Phred you look slightly to the left, and when you talk to Phelicia you look slightly to the right. Now, get rid of Phrank, but leave Phred and Phelicia exactly where they are, and instead of talking *to* them you talk *for* them. When you speak Phred's lines you look slightly to the left, and when you speak Phelicia's lines you look slightly to the right. This gives the audience the illusion of the two characters talking to each other.

One of the biggest mistakes neophyte oral interpretation performers make is to put the characters' foci too far apart. I have seen performances in which the student puts the two characters at full profile to the audience. This wide placement of focus turns the oral interpretation performance into a dance recital as the performer spins rapidly back and forth between each line of dialogue. It does create a comic effect, but even if the dialogue is a comedy, the audience should laugh at the piece, not the performer.

If a dialogue has more than two characters in it, the performer should create more points of focus and use one for each character. Remember, they should not be so far apart as to cause an unintended comical effect. And of course, for any dialogue the performer will want to do more to differentiate the characters than just give each character a separate point of focus.

Gestures

Put your hands in your pockets and keep them there. Now have a long conversation with someone. How does it feel? Most people can have a conversation without using their hands if they make a conscious effort to do so, but most people also find it far more natural to use gestures when they talk. *Gestures* add a lot of meaning to the words a person speaks. The lack of gestures is telling as well.

Gestures may not have as much power to communicate as the eyes or face do, but gestures are overt actions and are noticed more than the subtler facial expressions. Movement draws attention. Every movement the performer makes with her hands will draw the attention of the audience, so a performer must be aware of what she is doing with her hands. The performer can consciously include some specific gestures in her performance and then allow others to occur unconsciously. Like all of the performer's nonverbals, some gestures unconsciously added in rehearsal become conscious parts of her performance.

Posture

Posture is yet another aspect of the performer's visual communication. Should the performer stand up straight, slump, lean to one side, put her weight on one leg, bend in the middle? What do those postures communicate about character, about the piece being performed? Like most of our nonverbal communication, posture is an unconscious function. The next time you are sitting in a meeting, look at the seated posture of your colleagues around the table. What are their postures saying? A performer's posture should take on the general tone or attitude of the piece being performed.

Movement

"Should I stand in one place, or move around?" The question was put to me by one of my oral interpretation students who was new to performance. I told her that the piece of literature she was trying to perform was her best guide. She should try *movement* and see if it would work with her piece. She read through the first stanzas of her poem and paced back and forth as she did so. It did not work with the piece, but it was a breakthrough for her as a performer. It was the first time she had experimented with movement—or any nonverbals, for that matter—as she rehearsed. By the time she got to the performance, she included movement. She would move to one side for a few steps, then stop abruptly as if she was uncertain. I do not recall the poem she was performing, but the movement worked with the piece.

Whole body movement, like gesture, calls attention to itself and is one of the more overt forms of visual communication. As a performer, you do not want to throw whole body movement out of your bag of tricks, but you do want to be aware of it. Make sure it is adding to your performance, not taking away.

Visual Communication Exercises

- Of Mind and Mirror. Pick a poem, pick a partner, get a mirror. Perform a poem for your partner. Even if you have not had a chance to rehearse it, perform it for them. Your partner gets to hold the mirror. Anytime your partner wants to, she says "Freeze." You immediately freeze. Do not move a muscle. Do not change anything. Then your partner says "Think." You try to imagine what your face looks like at that moment. Then your partner says "Look" and holds up the mirror for you to look at your face and see if it is anything like you imagined. A variation on this is for your partner to say an emotion, like "Happy!" You try to put on a face that says "happy" and again imagine what it looks like. After you think you have achieved "happy," your partner holds up the mirror for you to see if what you imagined your face looked like is congruent with the reality. The purpose here is not to learn how to make certain emotions appear on your face, but to see if you know what your face looks like at any given moment.

- The Visually Rote Performance. For this exercise we will borrow a term that usually refers to a vocal phenomenon and apply it to the visual. In a *vocally* rote reading, the performer tries to read without any variation in the paralanguage. For this exercise you will first perform the piece with as much vocal variation as you can but be rote *visually*. In other words, read the piece with great vocal expression, but do not move a muscle otherwise. No facial expressions, no gestures, no posture changes, no movement, nothing. Try it. How did it feel? Now try it and perform it with both vocal and visual expression. How did it feel? What is the difference?

- The Mirror Teleprompter. Get a large hand mirror, something about the size of a piece of binder paper. Get a dry-erase marker. Find a short poem and write it on the mirror. Grimace and try to read the whole poem through the grimace, watching your face as you read. Smile as big as you can and read the poem again. Watch. Raise your eyebrows and open your mouth as wide as you can. Read again. What are you learning about your face? (By the way, I really hope you like your face!)

- Digital Recording. Record your performance digitally. Play it back and turn off the sound. What do you learn about your visual communication?

- The Eyes Still Have It. This is a variation on the "eye contact contests" we have all played. You know what I mean—the game where we see who can look the other person in the eye the longest without blinking or looking away. Memorize a few lines of a poem. Stare your partner in the eye and perform the poem, then let your partner perform it for you. It is not a contest but watch what happens to your partner's eyes when she performs. A variation on this is to perform a piece and have someone record your face in the camera's close-up mode. If the person can record just your eyes, all the better. Play it back and watch without the sound. What does your face do when you perform? What do your eyes do?

- Body Tape. Use the digital camera to record yourself performing but cut off your head in the viewfinder. Play it back and see what your body does apart from facial expression. Play it back in fast-forward mode to see if your movement is repetitious.

- Posture Play. Perform a short piece maintaining various postures. Perform standing erect. Perform slumped over. Perform while putting weight on one foot and leaning to the side. Lift one shoulder up and put the other down. The goal is learning to be in touch with your body as you perform.

- Gesture-matic. Perform a short piece and be visually rote except for one arm. Try to put all the visual communication of the piece into that one arm. Then use both arms but keep your elbows locked to your sides. Use one hand from the wrist only.

Chapter 6

Excellent Rehearsal Equals Excellent Performance

Creating a High-Quality Performance

IMAGINE GOING DOWN TO THE RUNNING TRACK and watching an athlete run the hurdles. The athlete is incredible, like poetry in motion. Each hurdle is leapt over with the grace and skill of a gazelle.

Imagine going to see a concert violinist. The musician's bow and fingers dance across the strings of the instrument and the music celebrates through the air like golden leaves of grace.

Imagine an actor performing a long monologue. By the end of the piece, you have laughed and cried, and your heart and mind feel cleansed.

When you see that kind of excellence, you do not find yourself thinking, "Gosh, I bet this is the first time they've ever done this." No, of course not. In fact, if you think anything at all it is to wonder how many hours of careful practice and rehearsal the individuals had to put in to become so proficient. When you see an excellent performance in sports or on the stage, you know those athletes and performers have worked long and hard to be that good.

You and I live in the academic world where we like to kick around the postmodern idea that all truth is relative and there are no absolutes. But there are some absolutes, and one of them is this: *High-quality anything takes time and effort.* From relationships to careers to material things to performance, if you want it to be good, then it will take time and effort. This is no less true for the oral interpretation performer.

There is a popular myth in amateur theater circles. According to this myth, a bad dress rehearsal means a good opening night. Nothing could be further from the truth. Usually, a bad dress rehearsal leads to a mediocre opening night, but it looks so much better than a bad dress rehearsal that everyone involved is relieved. Those involved like to say, "Don't worry. The show will come together." Buzzzzz, wrong, thank you for playing. A performance will not come together unless the people involved make it come together.

Your oral interpretation performance will not be good unless you take the time and do the work to make it good. Time and again I have seen students—and they were capable performers—toss off a poorly rehearsed piece and do a passable job. They settled for mundane when they could have been awesome.

High-Quality Performance Starts with High-Quality Material

Have you read a movie review that says the actors were good but could not save a bad script? Have you seen one of those movies? I recently watched a comedy about two lifelong fishing buddies and their latest misadventures. The actors in the film were both well-known, high-quality performers, but the script was dumb. It was not funny. In fact, I found myself feeling sorry for the actors because they had to be in this turkey. In any kind of performance—a movie, a play, an oral interpretation—if the words are not high quality, then the performance will be mediocre at best.

You must start with high-quality material if you hope to achieve an excellent performance. This is the key reason I do not let my students use the Internet as a source of material. If it is published only on the Internet, then I do not allow them to use it. If it is published in hard copy form, then at the very least you know that some editor somewhere thought it was good enough to risk publication. Take a moment, go back, and review the material I covered in Chapter 3 on selecting high-quality literature.

Now that you recall the whys and wherefores of selecting high-quality literature, there are a couple of other things to consider in the selection process. First, it is important for the performer to pick a piece she likes. If you are at least a little bit excited about the piece, then you will be able to convey that excitement to the audience. You should enjoy the selection process; it should not be a chore. If it feels like a chore, if it is like one more piece of homework you need to do, then try to change that attitude. Find ways to make the selection process fun.

Suppose you have an assignment to perform poetry, but you have not had much exposure to poetry and do not know where to start. At this point

I am sure it seems like work, but you can make it fun if you want to. See it as an adventure. You are now going to learn where the poetry is kept in the library, and you can go spend a couple of hours there browsing the stacks. A couple of hours—yikes! You are laying the foundation for a performance that you hope will touch the hearts and minds of your audience. Maybe you could make a date out of it. Send a note to that special someone to meet in the poetry section of the library, and make it sound mysterious. When she gets there, enlist her help in finding a piece. Make a game of it. (Maybe you could look for some romantic works.)

Another way to involve relationships in this process is to ask a significant other if they have a favorite poem or poet. Ask your best friends about what they know of poetry. Call your mom and enlist her help. Call your high school English teacher or your current English teacher and recruit her help. Check out a bunch of poetry books and have a reading-poetry-aloud party in your room.

Whatever you do, try to find a *personal connection* to the piece chosen. Either you like it, or someone you like helped you find it, or someone who holds a special place in your life recommended it. Do whatever it takes to make the process of selection an enjoyable experience.

You want to start the *rehearsal process* excited about the prospect of sharing this piece with the audience. If the piece you pick moves you, stirs your heart and mind, then you have good potential for bringing it to your audience in a manner that will move them.

You should start this *selection process* well before your performance date. Even for a short performance, one that might be three to five minutes in length, you should have your piece *selected at least a week in advance*. That means you would need to *start* the selection process about ten days in advance. It is critical that you give yourself the time needed to rehearse the piece well.

When striving for excellence, any performer needs to be dedicated to the rehearsal process, and that dedication starts with good planning. Once you have the piece selected, you need to plan the rehearsal process. You need to create a rehearsal schedule.

In general, it is better to have numerous short rehearsal sessions than a few long ones. Many short rehearsal sessions provide an opportunity for the piece to seep into your mind and heart. This kind of rehearsal schedule has a meditative quality to it. As you rehearse several times a day for fifteen or twenty minutes, you will begin to have a deeper understanding of the piece. You will find new meaning that was there all along, though you had yet to recognize it. As you come back to the piece over and over throughout the course of a day or a week, what it means to you will grow and change. You will make new discoveries about the piece. This kind of growth by discovery is less likely to happen with fewer, longer rehearsal sessions.

One way to enhance this discovery process is to make a copy of the piece and take it with you wherever you go. Then, whenever you have a few odd moments, waiting for class to start or standing in line somewhere, you can read over the piece and reflect on it.

Your personal rehearsal schedule should also include the rehearsal location. This is a crucial consideration because you need to be able to rehearse aloud. Reading the piece silently is not rehearsal. You are not going to perform silently. *Rehearsal* means getting ready to do something as it will be done in performance. If you are not rehearsing aloud, then you are not rehearsing.

Imagine a baseball player who wants to become a pitcher. She goes to her coach and explains this desire. Her coach tells her to sit on the bench and imagine pitching—all the different kinds of pitches and pitching the perfect game. So the player does. Day after day, she sits on the bench and imagines pitching. That is all she does: she imagines pitching. Then, the day of the first game arrives. The coach sends the player out to the mound with the admonition to throw the ball just like she did in her imagination. How well do you think that player is going to do? So too, is it with your rehearsal process. It will not be enough to hear the words in your head. You must speak the words aloud.

Thus, the performer needs a rehearsal space where she will not bother anyone, and she will not feel self-conscious as she rehearses aloud. The rehearsal space must be one that allows the performer to experiment freely without feeling inhibited. Of course, it is one thing to read aloud in a dorm room and quite another to shout. If the performance is going to have some very loud moments in it, then the rehearsal space needs to accommodate the volume. You will be trying out various paralanguage effects in rehearsal—maybe a high-pitched squeaky voice, followed by a low stuttering sound, and then some staccato shouting. The performer must have a rehearsal space where she can feel free to play, experiment, create, and make mistakes.

A rehearsal space that meets these qualifications may be hard to find, but on the typical college campus there are some possibilities. The theater and music buildings may have rehearsal rooms. Another less obvious choice is an empty classroom. Many colleges leave the classrooms open throughout the day and well into the night. The ideal place to rehearse would be the space in which you will perform. Not only will the performance space accommodate the rehearsal needs, but rehearsing there will help you to become comfortable performing that piece in that space.

Discovery—the First Step in Rehearsal

Every rehearsal session is a combination of discovery and experimentation, but it is helpful to think of discovery as the primary goal of the first few rehearsals. In the initial stages of rehearsal, you should try to let the literature speak to you. You want to hear what it has to say with no preconceived ideas.

First, the performer needs to make sure she understands what all the words mean denotatively. She also needs to know the connotative meanings that may exist in the context the literature creates. For example, one denotative meaning of "bats" is the flying mammal. But at the connotative level "bats" may also refer to someone's wacky state of mind. If the performer is unsure of the denotative meanings of any of the words in her piece, then she should look them up immediately.

Understanding the words is understanding the piece at a cognitive level, but the performer wants to understand it affectively too. During the first few read-throughs, the performer should be in touch with her feelings. What is her emotional response to this literature? What kinds of images does she get in her head when she reads it? What does it make her think about?

Does the piece resonate in the performer's *spirit* or *soul*? *Resonance* is a word that describes a sound-wave phenomenon. If I play a note on a stringed instrument, the sound waves will cause the strings of another nearby instrument to vibrate, to resonate. Does the piece of literature you are rehearsing and performing have content that causes a resonance in your spirit or soul?

Keeping a rehearsal journal may be helpful. After each rehearsal session, take a few moments and write down your feelings and impressions about the literature you are working on and about your rehearsal process. Record the details of your rehearsal process, e.g., "I rehearsed in the classroom for twenty minutes. I experimented with paralanguage, trying to create the sound of wind, as I read the description of the dust storm."

I sometimes require my students to keep a rehearsal journal and turn it in when they perform. I suspect that most of them have not realized it is meant to be a tool for them, not an assignment for my sake. If nothing else, the rehearsal journal helps the performer think more deeply about the piece she is rehearsing, and the rehearsal process itself. Reviewing the rehearsal journal before each new rehearsal can help the performer better understand the whole rehearsal/performance process.

Listen and Learn

Another rehearsal technique that is useful is to listen to the literature without seeing or reading the words. After all, the audience is going to hear the piece, not read it, so why not experience it as the audience will? Hearing the words without seeing them changes the channel of communication and gives the performer a different perspective that is useful as she prepares to perform.

You can ask someone else to read the piece to you. The reader, of course, will add some paralanguage to the words, and it is useful to hear how another person interprets the piece. As an in-class exercise, I have made my students perform the same short piece. It is often useful for them to hear and see the different kinds of nonverbals that other students add to the work. You, too, can ask a classmate to perform the piece she is working on, with you as the only audience member. The performer could also get a roommate or friend to simply read it to her. In either instance, the performer experiences the piece in a new way which may give her new insights into it and new inspiration about how she will perform it.

I recall rehearsing a scene from *The Glass Menagerie* in a summer acting workshop. As a class exercise, my partner and I switched roles and read the scene to each other. It was a little odd, because she was now reading the part of the gentleman caller and I was reading for Laura. But despite the gender changing, I learned new things about the gentleman caller. Acting and oral interpretation have enough similarities that the performer may well have the same kind of experience by having someone else read the piece aloud to her.

Another possibility is to record it and play it back. In fact, one way to become very familiar with your piece is to make an audio recording and then play it back as you drive, walk, or fall asleep. The one danger here is that you will tend to learn the paralanguage used in the recording, but if you remember that the rehearsal process is one of experimentation and growth, then you will retain the freedom to make changes as you progress.

I recommend recording the piece as you rehearse it and playing it back to yourself on a regular basis. At the very least you should listen to your recorded performance in the last one or two rehearsal sessions before the performance. Recording and playing back, more than anything else, will help you hear and fix the weaknesses of your performance.

Chapter 7

Heart Creates Art

Creatively Creating Performance, Part I

I BEGIN THIS CHAPTER WITH A POEM I wrote titled "A Poem on the Classroom Floor."

It died by dissection,
Its alliteration all
Spilled out like a slippery simile that
Tried to slither away from the analytical knife.
An explosion of metaphors scattered the room
Becoming debris from a war on words.
The rhymes, assigned their schemes of letters
. . . A, B, A, B, C, D, E, D, E, C . . .
Pulled away and pushed apart, lay as entrails,
"Untimely ripped" from the mother corpse.
It had life once.
Lovers have set its words to heart and
Cooed them into the ears and lips of romantic life.
Its author never thought of poetry as a hammer and nail
Kind of pursuit.
There was no blueprint for this poet to lay pen to.
But formula-like, a blueprint was applied.
And like a backwards carpenter the poem was taken apart.
And its pieces scattered about for inspection.
In the dissection process, no one noticed when the poem died.
There was no funeral in Literary Analysis 101 today.
They left the poem on the floor dead.
Without its life, no one wanted it anymore.

First, I must apologize to the English teachers of the world. Of course, many of them do not do what this poem describes. In fact, many English teachers know how to use literary analysis to bring a poem to life, not to kill it. But I have sat in the classrooms of some English teachers who analyze literature to death. I have sat in oral interpretation classes where we spent more time on literary analysis than on the rehearsal process. I have watched firsthand as poems, novels, and plays have been killed and butchered at the hands of fanatic professors who thought it was more important to identify each instance of assonance or correctly identify the point of view than to try to experience the meaning of the literature.

Literary analysis for the sake of literary analysis has no useful purpose and is a waste of time. On the other hand, literary analysis for the sake of understanding and more fully experiencing literature is very useful and may even be a wonderful rehearsal process tool. But I am not going to cover all the ins and outs of literary analysis. There are plenty of English literature textbooks that cover the material far more adequately than I can here. If the performer is serious about performance—especially oral interpretation or acting—she should see to it that her education includes the basic elements of literary analysis.

One thing to think about in this regard is the approach a writer takes to her work. In most instances, a writer does not think in the terms of literary analysis as she writes. When a poet is inspired to write a poem, she does not think, "Okay, I'll start with some alliteration, then I'll go through three metaphors and an oxymoron. Then after some synecdoche and assonance I'll end with a simile." No. I am confident in asserting that poets do not think that way when they write a poem. Poets write poems they feel inspired to write. Sure, most poets who are of publishable quality can identify all the elements of literary analysis, and they may even add some alliteration or change a simile to a metaphor as they rewrite and edit. But they make those changes because it makes the poem better, not because literary analysis calls for it. The poem itself comes from their hearts without a thought to literary analysis. The one exception would be when a poet writes in a specific form. A sonnet is not a sonnet unless it meets the denotative definition of "sonnet." The same is true with a haiku; it must meet the specific definition of that form. But even in those cases, the inspiration for the poem does not come from the form. The form is imposed on the poem; the inspiration comes from life. Or take for example the playwright. She knows that she will be limited to dialogue rather than narration. She knows she will not be writing any long narrative descriptions in her play. But again, the form is imposed on the inspiration; the inspiration does not come from the form.

Most writers of great literature write via a process of creative discovery. As the performer prepares an oral interpretation, she, too, should prepare via a process of creative discovery. So the emphasis in this textbook is on oral interpretation as a process of creative discovery as opposed to a process of technical analysis.

Creation in Rehearsal

As noted above, the oral interpretation performer is adding nonverbal communications to the verbal already supplied by the author. The creative process for the oral interpretation performer is in deciding how to use nonverbal communications to enhance the literature. Thus, the performer must make choices about the use of nonverbals as part of the rehearsal process. Some of these choices are directed by the literature.

The literature can direct the performer's choices in obvious ways. Descriptions of actions and emotions will direct nonverbal performance choices. For example, suppose the piece includes lines like "She felt incredibly sad" or "he shouted" or "the brook babbled in a low happy murmur." In these cases, it is clear what the nonverbal effect should be. If the character is sad, she should sound sad. If he shouts, then the performer should shout. If the brook is happy and babbling, then that should be represented in the nonverbal choices the performer makes. The performer will make some of these choices consciously, as in specifically choosing to shout when the character does. The performer will make other choices more intuitively. How does one sound like a babbling brook when performing a poem?

Other directions about nonverbals are less obvious in the literature. This ambiguity is especially true in plays. Occasionally a playwright will include a stage direction that suggests how a line should be performed, but that is rare. For the most part, as the performer prepares an oral interpretation performance of a play, she will have to read carefully, think critically, and feel freely to comprehend the emotions of the characters. In theater, actors and directors frequently call this "subtext," meaning that the connotation is underneath the words. Whole books are written on the idea of subtext, so I will not explore it in depth here. It would be worth the effort to go to the library, check out some books on play analysis, and spend time in the chapters that deal with the dialogue.

Sometimes you will not have much direction from the piece and will have to make nonverbal choices simply to keep the piece interesting. I have a poem I like to perform for my class about a man who collects things. Part of the poem is a long list of all the things he collects. Apart from the fact that the man enjoys all the things he collects, there are not many clues in the piece as to what kind of nonverbals I should add to the words. So I decided to "rate change." I start reading the list at a below-average reading speed, and I increase the speed until I am reading as fast as I can by the end. (I work very hard to keep my articulation clear in the fast part.) As I read the list, I take a purposeful pause when I run out of breath and make it obvious that I only stopped to take the breath. By the end of the piece, I am panting as if I was winded. Again, there is nothing in the piece to suggest that I perform it in this manner. I could make many other choices, but this is the one I like.

It Is More than the Words

Jill came to the front of the class to perform her first oral-interpretation-of-poetry assignment. She gave a brief introduction that concluded with, "Now, I want you all to close your eyes."

I quickly called a time-out. "Why do you want us to close our eyes? Shouldn't we be seeing what you perform?"

"Well, in this poem it's all in the words," Jill said.

"If that were true, then we should be reading the poem, not watching you perform it for us. If you truly believe that in this poem it's all in the words, then you should have picked another poem, one in which you don't think it's all in the words, so that you'll have something to perform."

"Oh."

Because this was Jill's first attempt at oral interpretation, I gave her a couple more days to rehearse her piece before she performed it for us— with our eyes open. But it was a good lesson for her and for the class. You must remember that the performance is always more than just the words. If the impact the performer is trying to create can be created via the words alone, then why perform it? In that case, the audience would do better to read the piece.

There is not any literature in the world that cannot be performed because it is "all in the words." There is literature so powerful that you may think it is a mistake to try to perform it, that it would be better just to let the audience experience it via the personal process of reading. That is a choice you would have to make in the selection process. Personally, I love bringing the most powerful literature I can to my audience. A good performance will add something to any piece of literature, but a bad performance can take something away.

Exercises in Creative Rehearsal Process

These exercises are only a starting point. The performer should work toward letting her own creative ideas inspire the rehearsal process. These exercises are not in any specific order. There is no magic here. It is just a matter of breaking loose, learning to take risks, trying to create. These exercises may or may not help. This is art. No one knows if any of the answers are right or not. But then, art is not about right answers.

- Create a rote reading. Be as nonverbally neutral as possible. Read the piece with no changes in paralanguage, no facial expressions, no body movement—nothing. Be as robotic and computerlike as possible. Record the rote reading. Listen to it. Read the piece backward in the rote mode. As you read in the rote manner, mentally note any urges to do more with it. Use those urges as starting points to experiment with the piece.

- Jump back to the previous exercises in vocal and visual nonverbal communications. Combine two or more of the exercises so you are playing with paralanguage and body language simultaneously.

- Go to the photography section of the library. Find a book of portraits. Randomly pick some photos and read your piece to the picture. How would the person in the picture sound if he or she were reading the piece? Find a picture of the person you think would most likely speak the piece from the heart.

- Go to the zoo. Read your piece to the animals. Read your piece as if an animal were reading it. What kind of animal would select and read your piece?

- Create different voices for any dialogue that takes place in the piece. You can also try different voices for the whole piece. How does the piece sound in a low, slow voice? A squeaky, fast voice? A voice that shouts when you should whisper and whispers when you should shout? Watch some of actor Robin Williams's films for inspiration on voices. *Good Morning, Vietnam,* and *Mrs. Doubtfire* are especially good in this regard.

- Perform the piece backward, trying to keep the same nonverbal choices you made when you read the piece forward.

- Spell the words of the piece out loud, again trying to keep the same nonverbal choices.

- Perform the piece in a variety of environments: Hide under the covers of your bed and perform the piece. Perform the piece in the shower. Perform it in the middle of an empty sports field. Perform it in the closet, in a car, in a concert hall, in a hallway.

- Try to rehearse your piece to as many different people as possible. Call your mom and perform it for her over the phone. Call someone's answering machine and perform it for the machine. Perform it into a computer and send the audio file to everyone on your e-mail list.

- Perform your piece with background music. Try some rock, then country western, then classical, then pop, then hip-hop, then punk—you get the idea. You probably will not want to use background music when you perform for an audience, but there may be circumstances where that is an okay choice.

- Dress up in your Sunday best and perform it. Try it in your grungiest clothes. Try it naked (alone and in private, of course).

These exercises are just some of the ideas that will take you into the process of discovery. The goal is to create a performance that works for the performer, for that piece, and for that audience. As the performer gets closer and closer to the actual performance, her experimentation will become less and less. She will finalize the choices she makes about the nonverbal elements. The performer will create a performance that has a great deal of similarity from one rehearsal to the next, and yet part of her goal is to create something that seems fresh and vitally new each time she performs it.

While a performance should be well-rehearsed and under the control of the performer, there is something to be said for taking a risk if you get some inspiration. I was performing a short monologue about a guy who was up the whole night before. I had settled on my performance choices and was ready to go. Then, even as I was stepping onto the stage for my first performance, it occurred to me that I should start with a yawn. After all, the character was up all night. So I did, and it worked well. This is art. Take the risk.

The Properties of Props: A Pear Is a Pear Is a Pear

Alice brought us a poem about a pear. At the outset of her piece, she set a pear, with a leaf still attached, on the lectern and left it there for the duration of her performance. She pointed to it a couple of times. I was a student at the time and did not think much about it. She performed well, and we enjoyed the poem.

Then, Eric performed a poem about bells, and he brought a couple of bells along to illustrate the sounds. He had some sleigh bells and a couple of hand bells to illustrate different tones. This time, I was the teacher, so I had to consider the effect of his props on the overall piece. His performance brought to my class the question of whether *props* are a legitimate part of an oral interpretation performance.

Some definitions of oral interpretation prohibit the use of props. I have never seen props used in an oral interpretation competition, but that does not mean they are not allowed or that no one ever uses props. I have never had a professor address the question in class, and in all the research I did and books I read before starting this book, I did not uncover any content in this area. If the performer is in a class or a competition in which the powers that be say that props may not be used, then my best advice is not to use them. In all other cases, the performer must decide if she wants to use props, and she must carefully weigh the effect of using props on the performance. Like all other performance choices, the use of props can add to or take away from the performance, depending on the circumstances.

One semester my oral interpretation class got into a "prop phase." It started when one of the students used her script as a prop, then one performer threw a deck of cards in the air at an appropriate moment in the piece. The most fun was a young man who did a piece about a couple "parking." It was a humorous dialogue, and at one point he reached into his shirt and pulled out a bra. It worked well and brought the house down in laughter.

Other instances of prop use did not work so well, as best illustrated by the girl who spent five minutes littering the stage with toys before she read her poem about toys. She did not use any of the toys specifically. They were just there. It did not add to the piece, and the time it took to litter them about and collect them afterward took away from her performance.

Here are my best recommendations about using props: First, keep it simple. The props themselves should be simple, and their use should be simple. Large, complicated props or elaborate, intricate movement with props should usually be avoided. The props should not detract focus from the overall impact of the performance. "Simple" also means using only a few props. I have seen oral interpretation performances that were so laden with props that all I remember are the props, not the performance.

Second, just like all other performance choices you make, once you use a prop in rehearsal, do not feel locked into its use. Try it out, and if it does not seem to work, then get rid of it. This is one area where videotaping and watching your rehearsal is valuable.

The bottom line is a question of aesthetic judgment. Use props only if you truly think they add to the performance, only if you think they make it better.

Costumes: Tell Me the Truth, How Do I Look?

Costumes fall under the same guidelines as props, but the question of costumes brings up the question of general appearance. The oral interpretation performer must think of her general appearance as part of the performance. A performer's clothes, haircut, and jewelry all affect how and what the audience perceives.

One rule of thumb is to ensure that your appearance does not distract from the performance. If your hair is dyed punk-rock green, then it may be a distraction for the audience as you try to perform a serious dramatic piece. Wearing clothes that have logos on them is generally not a good idea. Your favorite bright pink blouse may not be the best choice on performance day unless the piece you are performing has some bright pink elements in it. Do you normally wear a lot of dazzling hand and wrist jewelry? How will that affect your gestures? Will the jewelry distract? You must also ask that question of long dangly earrings. The longer the earrings, the more they will pull focus. Have well-tattooed arms? Long sleeves may be in order, depending on the nature of your performance piece.

It is always a good idea to dress up, at least a little, for a performance. If you normally wear a t-shirt to class, then performance day is the day to wear a collared shirt, and maybe even a tie. The performance is what the performer wants the audience to remember, not the logo on a t-shirt or a giant gold watch.

The performer can choose to dress in a way that enhances the performance. I recall Sylvia, whose favorite poet wrote very dark poems about suicide and death. When Sylvia, who normally dressed in bright colors, performed this poet for class, she let her hair hang down the sides of her face and wore a black sweatshirt and jeans. Her look worked well for that particular performance.

I recall Rob, who was doing a children's piece about barnyard animals. He wore bib overalls, tied a red bandana around his neck, and donned a straw farmer's hat. It was a costume that worked just fine for his piece.

Like props, there are some oral interpretation arenas where costumes are not allowed. If that is the case, you will want to stick to the strictures of the circumstances. If there are no strictures, keep the costuming simple, make sure it adds to the performance, and rehearse in costume so you know how it will affect the performance.

To Memorize or Not to Memorize, That Is the Question

Like teachers everywhere, I am constantly bombarded with advertisements for new textbooks and classroom videos, but over the years I have received only a few advertisements for classroom materials related to oral interpretation. So I was pleasantly surprised when I received promotional materials for a videotape about preparing an oral interpretation performance. I asked the audiovisual resource person on our library staff if she could get a perusal copy for me. She did. It was a well-produced video, and the content, for the most part, followed what I taught in my classroom for many years . . . until it got to the section on memorization. According to this resource, the performer should *always* memorize the piece, and then *pretend* that she is reading from the script.

Apparently, this is a bone of contention in some oral interpretation circles. I recently talked to a woman who coached a high school speech team. One of the competitions they regularly entered was in oral interpretation. She told me how her students had been penalized for memorizing their piece. She told me that in this competition they were required to carry a script *and* were required to turn pages.

The organizers of that competition may have been trying to draw a line between acting and oral interpretation. Suppose an oral interpretation performer chose a monologue from a play and memorized the piece. That performer is acting, not engaging in oral interpretation. On the other hand, if that did happen, then it is a simple matter for the judges to give it a poor score, because it crossed the line into a different performance genre.

I do not require my students to memorize their pieces, but I do expect them to know the work well enough that they do not stumble or lose their place. Yet, there is nothing wrong with memorizing a piece for oral interpretation. Just make sure you do not cross the line into acting. If you perform prose or poetry or nonfiction literature, then clearly that is not acting. If you select a piece from a play, then portray at least two characters, do not memorize it, and do not use costumes. Then you will safely stay within the definition of oral interpretation.

The bottom line here is this: if you do cross over into acting, so what? Unless it is a classroom setting that has strictures about staying in the oral interpretation mode, it does not matter so long as the audience has a good time.

A Performance-Friendly Script

Penny came late to her final. The assignment was to perform a four-to-six-minute oral interpretation from a genre of the student's choice. Penny had brought a large children's book. Her introduction was perfunctory, and she began to perform. Apparently, the children's book she was reading from was a picture book, with "picture" being the operative word. She never read more than a dozen words before she had to turn a page. Penny was a capable performer, but this was not a performance. It was an exercise in page turning. I had to give her a poor grade, and she knew exactly why she got it. She had not taken the time to create a performance-friendly script to work from, and that oversight damaged her final product. Part of the rehearsal process should be the creation of a script that enhances your ability to perform.

Many times, I have seen students work right from a novel or book of poetry. If the book is easy to handle, then there is nothing wrong with this choice. I once saw a young man win first place in an oral interpretation competition by reading directly from a volume of Carl Sandburg's poetry. The book fit in his hand nicely, and he only had to turn the page once during the performance. Holding the book in one hand, he gestured and moved about in a fluid polished manner. The book became a seamless part of his performance.

I have also seen many students damage their performance by using books that had a large format, were heavy, had too many pages to turn, or had pages that would not stay turned. I have watched as focus was detracted by too much page turning, lost pages, books that had to be held in two hands, and a couple of times, books that were so large and heavy that they were dropped—a real performance killer. Choosing to perform directly from a book is an attractive choice because it involves less effort than creating a simpler format. But do not let laziness be your guide. Taking the path of least resistance is not an active choice. If you choose to work directly from the book, make sure it is a choice that enhances rather than distracts.

Besides too much page turning, there are other ways the script can pull focus and hurt the performance. A book with a bright or colorful cover may not be a good choice. I have had students perform from a handful of loose-leaf pages. They struggle to keep the pages from going limp and sagging over their hand, or they have the pages in the wrong order and must fuss with them to find their place, or they drop a page, or they discover a page is missing. I have had students perform from a handful of loose-leaf pages stapled in one corner. They do not drop any pages, but they have all the same problems as those mentioned above. Plus, those who staple have the added problem of one or more flipped-over pages hanging from the end of their script, swinging back and forth, taking on a life of their own, pulling focus.

The best choice is to create a script that specifically meets the needs of your oral interpretation performance. You should start by photocopying the pages of the text you will work from. An even better choice is to take a few moments at the computer and word-process the piece. Typing a piece into the computer will cause you to see the words in a more intense way, almost like meditating on them. Also, a word-processed piece makes it easy for the performer to do any passage she wants and still have a clean script. Regardless of whether you word-process or photocopy, you want to have several copies of the piece to work from in the rehearsal process.

Next, get a standard three-ring binder in a neutral color. Black is best, but any solid color will do. The performer should avoid bright, cheery colors if she is performing a somber piece. The binder should have a narrow spine, say an inch or less. I prefer a half inch. It should also have solid sides, not the floppy plastic type. Three-hole punch all the copies of your piece and put them in the binder.

As you work on the piece, you can create your own shorthand for marking your paralanguage choices. You can indicate pauses, words you want to emphasize, places where you want to increase volume or change voice types. When I perform a drama selection, I like to word-process the piece, cutting out all the stage directions. Then, I use a different color highlighter for each character to help me keep them separate as I perform. Whatever you do, feel free to mark all over your first copy. Remember, it is a creative process, and you will make changes as the performance grows, probably many changes. When the first copy is so marked up that you can hardly read it anymore, start with the second copy. Transfer your shorthand to the second copy, keeping only those choices you like, then throw the first copy away and continue the rehearsal process. You may go through three or four copies of the piece before you finalize your performance script. The goal is to arrive at a final version that is clean and neat with only those markings you have decided to keep.

The Virtual Performance

If you have followed all the steps above, then you are well prepared. Your script is ready, you have explored the piece fully, and crafted a creative performance. Now you are ready for your last few sessions of rehearsal. Your goal is to make the last few rehearsals as close to performance conditions as possible. You should use the script you will use in performance, wear the same clothes you will wear in performance, and use whatever props, if any, you will use in performance. If possible, go to the place where you will perform and engage in the last rehearsals there. If you make these last few rehearsals as close to performance conditions as possible, there will not be any surprises when you actually perform.

Timing Is Everything

Well, maybe it is not everything, but it is an important consideration of your rehearsal process. You should know the length of your performance.

If the performance is to fulfill an assignment in an oral interpretation class, you will almost always have time guidelines imposed by the instructor. I usually give my students a two-minute window, as in "three to five minutes" or "four to six minutes." If the length of your performance is less than the minimum requirement for a class assignment, then you have not met the minimum standard for the assignment. It would be like not meeting the minimum page requirement for a written assignment. If your performance is a lot longer than the maximum, then you can throw the class off schedule, since the class will most likely need to get through a certain number of performances each day. In either case, going under time or over time, your grade may suffer. I usually grade harder on those who are under time than those slightly over time. In my classroom, if performers are seriously over time, then I interrupt and ask them to stop. I would much rather have my students present well-rehearsed, polished, entertaining performances that barely meet the minimum time requirement than go over time with a rambling, poorly rehearsed, uncreative piece.

Length of performance remains a serious consideration when the performance is outside the classroom. In these cases, you will need to weigh the circumstances of the performance and make an intelligent estimate as to what is an appropriate length. For example, when I perform for local fundraising events and talent shows, there is usually a vague suggestion about length. The contact person will say something like, "The theme is the joy of Christmas, and we are looking for performances that are five to ten minutes long." If I am reading a Scripture passage in church, then the length of the passage determines the length of the performance. If I am performing a piece as part of a lecture or speech, I usually have a specific piece I want to perform related to the content, so again the piece dictates the length. In those rare circumstances where I have been allowed to perform as long as I want, I have had to determine what was reasonable given the audience and the circumstances.

Whatever the case, about halfway through the rehearsal process you should begin timing the performance. If it is too long, then you should first consider shortening your introduction. Introductions should be kept short anyway. If the introduction is as short as possible and the performance is still too long, then you will have to cut the piece. The key to this kind of cutting is to keep the most interesting parts of the piece.

If the performance is too short, the best choice is to add more literature. Do a longer passage from the novel or play. Add one more poem on the same theme or by the same author. It is a mistake to lengthen the piece by making the introduction longer.

And in This Corner . . . the Introduction

Lydia got up to perform her prose fiction piece. She introduced it by sharing a few facts about the author and giving a brief synopsis of the storyline up to the point of her passage. Then she apologized to the class because the piece was about chastity, and she knew that "not everyone here believes in that." After Lydia performed, I asked her and the class about her introduction, especially the apology. Most of the students were noncommittal in their responses, but a few thought it was good that Lydia was not trying to push her beliefs on anyone else. I then pointed out that Jack had performed a piece that included R-rated profanity, Mary performed a piece that described the aftermath of a date rape, Mary Jane performed a piece that included the description of a woman having her head bitten off by an alien monster, and none of them apologized for anything. But here was Lydia apologizing for a piece that might have been promoting chastity.

What is wrong with this picture? At the very least, Lydia did not need to apologize for anything. In her effort to create a useful and interesting introduction, she told her audience too much about the content of the piece, and she worked against herself by assuming things about the audience and apologizing for her choices. When she performed the piece, it became clear that chastity was the theme. She should not have told us that in her introduction.

The *introduction* is an important part of the performance. While you do not perform the introduction in the same way you perform the piece itself, the introduction is nonetheless part of the performance, and you should treat it as such. About halfway through the rehearsal process, you should create the introduction, and then include it in every rehearsal.

The introduction should be as brief as possible, yet still get the job done. I can quote one of the best introductions to an oral interpretation performance I have ever heard. It went like this, "The Raven, by Edgar Allen Poe!" That was it. That is all Mike said. But he said it with perfect articulation and such force that it worked. He also had the advantage of choosing a piece that most of his audience already knew about.

The introduction should only include pertinent information. The name of the author and the title of the piece should be included. Also, if there is information needed for the audience to fully understand the piece that is not in the piece, then that information should be in the introduction. I once performed a poem about a Jewish man who was forced to play the piano to entertain Hitler. Those details were not explained in the poem, so I included them in the introduction. The introduction should include whatever information the audience will need to understand the piece at the cognitive level—no more.

In my example above about the Jewish pianist, it would have been a mistake for me to tell the audience that in the piece the word "dancer" meant the piano player and the word "clown" meant Hitler. Those are details that are learned from the performance of the poem, not its introduction.

The introduction is not a substitute for the piece. It should not do work or reveal information that the piece does or reveals itself. That was one of the mistakes Lydia made. The theme of the piece was chastity, but instead of telling us that in her introduction, she should have let us discover that through her performance. As much as possible, you should not tell the audience what the piece is about.

Suppose you do a piece about a father and daughter who have a love-hate relationship. It may be important to tell the audience that the two characters are a father and daughter if the biology of their relationship is not clear in the piece. But the audience should discover what kind of emotional relationship the two characters have via the performance of the work.

Anytime you perform a passage from a novel or short story, it is necessary to create a brief synopsis of the storyline up to the point where your passage begins. How much you do or do not tell in the synopsis is an artistic judgment you have to make. The key guideline is this: Anything that is revealed in the piece should not be part of the introduction. By "revealed in the piece," I mean revealed in any way.

Penelope did a piece about a guy who has a psychedelic vision while on drugs. Though psychedelic drugs are far from wonderful, her performance was. In her introduction, she made the correct choice of not telling us the man was on drugs. By the end of her performance, it was clear to the whole audience that the guy was in some kind of altered state of mind.

As much as possible, the introduction should not include information about emotions. You should not have to tell the audience what kind of emotions the work should evoke. I should not have to tell an audience that what I am about to perform will make them sad. The performance itself should create that response in the audience. If it does not, then either I have not performed well, or my understanding of the piece is poor. Telling the audience what kind of emotions I hope to evoke will not make up for my inability as a performer.

You should not have to explain the emotions of the characters in the piece either. If one of the characters in the piece is ecstatic with joy, then that joy should shine through the performance. One exception to this guideline is important information about previous emotional states. Suppose the character who expresses joy has previously experienced ten years of depression due to a personal tragedy. If that information is not revealed in the passage, it is important to include it in the introduction.

Get Their Attention

There are endless creative ways you can cause the introduction to function as an attention-getter. You can ask a rhetorical question: "Have you ever lain awake just before sunrise and wondered what the heck life is all about? See what answers you find in this passage from Phred Pharkel's *Eating the Earth Hole*." There, in two short sentences, you have aroused the curiosity of the audience and told them the author's name and the title of the piece—that is all they need to know. Or you could start the introduction with an off-the-wall quote from the piece. What if, before the performer said anything else, she said, "Dang! I have never seen a guy who could swallow that big a rock in one gulp!" before going on to give the author and title. Creative ways of getting the audience's attention in the introduction are limitless, and some may even involve violation of all the introduction guidelines I have set forth above. Remember that this is art, and there is no such thing as carved-in-stone rules.

The Pause

You will need to signal to the audience that the introduction is over, and that the performance is about to begin. The simplest way to accomplish this is to pause between the introduction and the performance. This is like that moment in a theatrical production when the house lights go down and the curtain opens. The entire auditorium falls quiet. You will have that same quiet in that pause between your introduction and your performance. Do not trample over the pause. Make it a real pause, not just a hesitation. It should last two or three seconds, at least. Use that couple of seconds to make the transition from introducer to performer. Use that couple of seconds to mentally set your concentration on the work you are about to do.

Internal Introductions and Summaries

Sometimes you need to jump back into introduction mode in the middle of the performance. If you are performing pieces by more than one author, or even several pieces by the same author, then you may want to make a transition between the pieces by giving each its own introduction. You would follow all the same introduction guidelines noted above. You should include a pause both before and after these internal introductions.

Another reason to take a pause in the performance is the need for an internal summary. If the performer is reading several passages from the same short story or novel, then she may need to summarize the parts of the storyline that occur between the passages. The best place to put those summaries is often between the passages. The same general guidelines for introductions apply to these internal summaries.

Chapter 8

I Would Rather Die

Overcoming the Fear of Performance

RICHARD WAS CLOSE TO SEVEN FEET TALL, and he must have weighed nearly three hundred pounds. Every inch of him was muscle. A jagged scar started at the top left side of his forehead and danced its way down and across his face, ending under the right side of his chin. He was in prison for murdering a drug dealer. The local community college offered courses in Richard's prison, and I was one of the adjunct faculty. In this public speaking course, I started with a unit on oral interpretation. On the day of his first performance, Richard stood before the class with sweat pouring from his jagged brow, knees knocking, hands and voice shaking. This giant man with a body of steel, who had led gangs into street wars and clearly had suffered immense pain, was terrified to perform a poem for the class. And Richard was not the only one. Surveys indicate that many people are less afraid of dying than they are of public speaking. While public speaking and oral interpretation are two different genres of communication, the same fears are engendered by both. Knowing that many people have this fear helps a little, but not much. There are some steps you can take to work toward overcoming the fear of performance.

The first step in overcoming the fear of performance is to have a realistic understanding of that fear. When the thing you are afraid of remains an obscure and poorly defined thing, it is hard to deal with. Also, ambiguity about it makes you more afraid of it. Makers of horror movies have known and exploited this fear of the unknown for a long time. Suppose you go to see a horror movie. The first image of the film is little Kathy walking down the street bouncing a ball. The camera does a close-up of Kathy's face as she hums a little tune. Then there is a close-up of the bouncing ball. We get a shot of a spooky tree in front of a run-down house. The camera goes back to Kathy, then back to the tree. We get a shot as if we were in the tree watching Kathy. Back to the ball, back to the tree, back to up in the tree. The music starts going into some creepy low notes. The camera cuts to a shot of Kathy's ball going over the fence and landing by the tree. We cut to the view from the tree and see the ball rolling toward it. The music gets louder. Little Kathy opens the old creaky gate and starts toward the tree. The camera cuts back and forth between the tree and Kathy. The music gets louder. By now, we in the audience are screaming, "No. Leave the ball. Run, little Kathy, run!" Of course, the filmmakers still have not shown us what is hiding in the tree. It could be a soft little harmless kitten for all we know. But because we do not know, we are terrified. Fear of performance is like that: the performer is not sure of what is causing the fear, she just knows that she is afraid. So the first step is to get a realistic understanding of that fear.

The fear of performance does not involve being afraid of physical harm. Unless the performance involves some kind of circus skill, as with trapeze artists or high-wire walkers, there is little chance that you will come to bodily injury. The risk-management specialists for the companies that sell insurance to colleges and universities are not too concerned that students are performing poetry for each other in class. I have never heard of an oral interpretation student being injured during her performance. If there is one thing we know about this fear, is that it has nothing to do with being physically hurt. So that means it is a mental fear, a kind of phobia, like being afraid of the dark. The fear is in the performer's head and has more to do with the emotions than the body.

It Is in Everyone's Head

Some surveys show that 85% or more of all people are fearful about public speaking to one degree or another. And as noted previously, while public speaking and oral interpretation have real differences, they have similarities, too. When most neophytes perform, they experience some anxiety, and the anxiety increases as the performance gets closer.

My daughter Mandi and I entered a song-and-dance routine in a talent show. It was Mandi's idea, but she was so nervous before we went on that I thought I was going to have to call it off. It was one of her first performing experiences, but even now as a seasoned veteran of many performances, she still gets a little nervous. I do, too.

I remember the first day I stood outside a classroom full of college students who were expecting me to come in and teach them something. I was nervous. True, a college lecture is not a performance, but there are some similarities. I still get a little nervous and excited on the first day of class.

Even professional performers sometimes get nervous. I once worked with a guy who had spent many years playing supporting roles on Broadway. He told me that about halfway through his professional career he went through a period where he had horrible stage fright that came on suddenly for no apparent reason.

The point I am trying to make is that the fear of performance is normal. It is a common phenomenon. If the performer is nervous about getting up in front of the class and performing an oral interpretation, then she is not an oddball.

You have already done many hard-to-do things in life. You got into college; that is not so easy. You probably have learned to drive a car at speeds fast enough to snuff your life out in an instant if you lost control; that is no small accomplishment either. Hopefully most of you will have conjured up the courage, at least once in your life, to ask that special someone out on a date. You have passed swim tests, earned merit badges, gotten that first job, moved away from home for the first time, learned to run a computer. You have learned to do all kinds of things, and you can learn to overcome the fear of performance, as well. You can take the very first step right now.

I Think I Can, I Think I Can, I Think I Can

Remember the story about the little engine who succeeded in pulling a long train over the big hill by believing she could? That little engine was on the right track. The first step in being successful at anything is to believe that you can. If you had never believed that you would get into college, then you never would have applied. If you did not think you would be able to learn to drive a car, then you never would have tried. The first real step toward overcoming the fear of performance is to believe that you can.

I remember Tim. He was a student in one of my public speaking classes. After his last major speech, he sat down and muttered, "I've hated every minute of this." After class I asked him what was going on. I tried to debrief with him his whole approach to public speaking to see if I could help make it less painful for him. The bottom line for Tim was that he never chose to try to do anything about his hatred of public speaking. He had convinced himself that he would never like it, that it would always be a negative experience, that he would never be any good at it. The truth was that Tim was a decent public speaker. He had received a B on his last couple speeches. But Tim never had a vision of himself as doing anything but hating it, so his prophecy was self-fulfilling.

You can avoid the foibles that ensnared Tim. Even if you are seriously afraid of performance, you can begin to speak and act like you are not that afraid. Send an e-mail home today. It should go something like this: "Dad, I am writing to tell you how excited I am about my oral interpretation class. Our first performance will be next week, and I am really looking forward to it. I suppose I may be a little nervous, but I know I can handle it. Your capable son, Rich." Tell your roommate, tell your friends, tell your classmates, tell anyone you can that you are going to do well in your performances.

Begin to envision yourself as a successful oral interpretation performer. Actively imagine yourself having a successful performance experience. Imagine coming to class on the day of the performance, having rehearsed well, feeling confident and ready. Imagine being able to relax and enjoy the work of all the students who perform before you. Imagine that when it is your turn, you take the stage with confidence. You boldly begin the introduction, and your voice is strong and clear. Imagine the audience responding with laughter and tears. Imagine that they rise to their feet in uproarious acclaim when you finish. Imagine throwing up . . . No, wait, do not do that last one.

To be successful at anything, you must first believe that you can achieve success. I have worked with hundreds of students and have yet to see the one who could not overcome the fear of performance to a reasonable degree.

It is important to note that you are not trying to achieve perfection in this regard. Expect to be at least a little nervous. Even the most seasoned, most confident performer may be a little anxious right before a performance. In some cases, being absolutely confident and calm can work against you. I have watched as confident performers became overconfident and turned in poor quality performances as a result.

The Monster Has Cute, Blue Eyes

See if you can identify those aspects of performance that you specifically respond to with fear. Make a list. Title the list, "I am afraid of performance because I am afraid that . . ." Then make a list of specific concerns: "my hands will shake," "my voice will crack," "I will lose my place." See if you can identify the fear factor in the items on your list. So what if your hands shake? What will that hurt? If you lose your place, who cares? The sun will still come up tomorrow. What is it that underscores all this fear? Most likely it is that you will look like a fool in front of the audience. Bingo, that is it. For most people, the fear of performance is the fear of failure, the fear of rejection. Hang on to that thought for a moment and go back to the other things on your list.

Create a contingency plan to address each of your specific fears. Add a column to the right of your first list with your specific action plan. Across from "my hands will shake," write, "I'll hang on to my script with both hands, or I'll hang on to the lectern." Across from "I will lose my place," write, "I will take a breath, find my place, and go on." Do the same for all. Then plan on using your contingency, if needed. It works; I know from first-hand experience.

I love performing, and I enjoy singing, but I do not like to sing as part of a performance. I made the mistake of singing loudly in church once. Actually the mistake was not singing loudly—it was that I sang loudly when the lady who was directing the Easter musical was standing right in front of me. Before I could escape, I was recruited into the cast. I rehearsed a lot and was doing fine, but I was a little worried about my voice cracking with emotion. The song right before mine was seriously moving, and I was afraid that in the passion of the performance I would lose hold of my emotions. So I created a contingency plan. I decided that if my voice did crack, I would just speak the next couple of lyrics without singing them, and then sing again as soon as I could. I did fine until dress rehearsal. About halfway through my song, my voice cracked, but I enacted my contingency plan, and it worked fine. So create your contingency plans and be prepared to use them. Now, back to "the mother of all performance fears."

The Mother of All Performance Fears

The fear of performance is really the fear of rejection by the audience, the fear of failure. This is a legitimate fear, and you are right to be concerned about it. After all, the audience is there to see a performance. They are expecting it to be good, and if they have paid for their tickets, then they have a right to expect it to be good. But much of the oral interpretation you engage in will be in amateur settings where no one has paid. Let me try to put a face on that audience for you.

Remember when you had to go to a music recital, and you watched as some of the students were so nervous that they could hardly play? How about those class presentations where you watched as your classmates could barely stammer their way through a book report because they were afraid? As an audience member in those situations, how did you feel? What were you thinking? Did you have a feeling of superiority, knowing that you could do much better? Did you think, "Boy, this guy is really bad! What a loser!" No. Most likely your feelings were of empathy, and if you were thinking anything it was, "Man, I know exactly how that guy feels." Because the fear of performance is such a common occurrence, when the audience sees evidence of it, they understand completely and, for the most part, will not have a condemning attitude toward the performer. This is not to suggest that you should not strive to keep your nervousness under control. Even though the audience has not paid anything to watch you perform, you should still strive for a polished performance.

What the audience has a right to receive is different when they have paid to experience the performance. One wonderful aspect of performance is that if a performer gets to the point where she has a paying audience, then she probably has enough experience as a performer and enough rehearsal before her performance that even if she is nervous, it does not show.

For most people, the fear of performance lessens as they get more experience. Performing is like anything else that is difficult to do. Your first experience with it may be nerve-wracking and less than fun, but you learn from it. You try it again, and each time you are less afraid and you even start to enjoy performing. I recall the first time I realized that I enjoyed performing. It was in my second high school play. I only had a small part, and we only had two performances, but after coming offstage on opening night I felt exhilarated. You, too, can come to the point where you do not fear performance but look forward to it. Experience will help a lot in achieving that end.

Fear Can Be Good

It is not a good idea to expect to be totally free from all anxiety as you prepare for a performance. It is unreasonable to expect to be totally calm in all performance situations. You can have performed a piece a dozen times but never have performed it for someone close to you. You find out that a parent, friend, or relative is in the audience, and you become a little nervous. Suddenly, you have a special concern that this performance goes well. No matter how proficient you become at performance, sooner or later you will run into a circumstance that causes you to experience the fear of performance once again, and that is okay. You are learning how to handle that fear now, and you will be able to handle it then.

Being a little anxious about performance is actually a good thing: It can be a source of energy that empowers your performance. It can be the motivation to stay focused and concentrate on performing. What do you do when you perform a piece multiple times? How do you keep it fresh and new for each audience? A little anxiety can also help in that regard. Anxiety about performing can even be the thing that motivates your desire to perform. Does the woman who climbs Mount Everest do so because she is totally without fear? No, the risk factor makes it more thrilling. So too, with performance.

What Does It Take to Jump into a Pit of Rattlesnakes?

Suppose your best friend, Pat, calls and tells you to be ready for a surprise in ten minutes. He picks you up and drives you to the local airport. You climb into a small plane and before you know it, you are 10,000 feet in the air. Pat gives you a funny-looking backpack, and you put it on. Pat opens the door of the plane, tells you the backpack is really a parachute, and shouts, "Jump!" Would you?

Now, rewind: Pat calls and tells you about a special, surprise birthday present—parachuting lessons. Every Saturday for the next two months, you spend a couple of hours at the local airport learning from the experts. You learn how the chute works and how to put it on. You learn all the safety measures, especially how to work the backup chute. You learn how to exit the plane and practice jumping out several times with the plane still on the ground. You also do several practice jumps from a short tower. You learn everything you can about parachuting, and you practice everything you can, except for jumping out of a plane in the air. The big day comes. You are in the air. Your ripcord is attached to the plane so that you do not even have to pull it yourself. Pat opens the door and shouts, "Jump!" Do you jump?

What is the difference between the end results in these two scenarios? Most people would feel much more confident about jumping out of the plane at the end of the second scenario than at the end of the first. Why? What is the difference that brings about confidence? Most people feel confident about situations in which they believe they are in control, in which they have a reasonable degree of knowledge about what is going to happen.

Performance is no different. Rehearsing well leads to both feeling and being in control of the performance, which in turn adds up to confidence. Engaging in a well-planned, well-executed rehearsal process will go a long way toward providing the ability to overcome the fear of performance. If I gave you only one suggestion for overcoming the fear of performance, it would be rehearse!

But What if a Lion Is Chasing You through the Jungle?

Imagine you are strolling through the jungle. A lion steps out from behind a tree. He wears a dinner jacket and reads a menu. You peek over his shoulder and see that the main entree for the evening meal is you. You instantly have the "fight or flight" response. When we are scared, feel threatened, become afraid, we have involuntary bodily responses. Those bodily responses give us the energy to fight the threat or to run away—to fight or take flight. In the case of the lion, either choice will not do you much good.

When the threat is mental, not a threat of physical harm, you still have the same involuntary fight or flight response. In the case of performance, you probably should not fight the audience, and the whole point of performance is antithetical to running away. Nevertheless, the involuntary response works against you, and you need to be prepared to deal with it.

One involuntary response is a surge of adrenaline. The big "A" causes a surge of energy that is transmitted to every muscle in your body. Adrenaline is what makes your hands shake, your legs tremble, and your voice quiver. It is responsible for the butterflies in your stomach. It can cause you to speak faster and breathe faster, which can lead to your mouth drying out, and in extreme cases, it can cause dizziness. It makes you start to sweat even though you are not hot. All these involuntary results of an adrenaline surge work against you as a performer, but the effects of adrenaline can be lessened, and adrenaline can be made to work for you.

The most effective way to lessen the effects of adrenaline is to lessen the initial surge. The less afraid you are, the less adrenaline your body will release. The more you engage all the previously mentioned aspects of overcoming the fear of performance, the less you are afraid, and the less of an adrenaline rush you will experience.

The only thing you can do with excess adrenaline is to use it. If you are nervous enough about performance that you have extra adrenaline in the hours before you perform, then you can take a walk or a run or engage in any form of exercise. In the moments immediately before the performance, you are usually in the kind of situation in which launching into a series of jumping jacks is not a real choice. But you can do simple isometric exercises. Press your knees together, feel the muscle tension, and relax. Squeeze your hands tight and relax, or even tighten up your buns and relax.

One of the best things you can do with the adrenaline rush is to use the energy to empower the performance. You must be able to concentrate and specifically to be in touch with your energy surge. You must know you are going to control and use it. You must be prepared to use it, and that is mostly a function of your ability to concentrate.

Relax, Right Now

Being able to relax both physically and mentally can help you experience less of the physical effects of anxiety and overcome the fear of performance. The better you understand the fear, and the more you work to build confidence, the less fear you will have to deal with and the more easily you can relax as you approach a performance.

There are other active things you can do to learn to relax. Your body is an amazing instrument, and you can train it to do many incredible things. Just like the athlete trains her body to glide over the high hurdles like a gazelle, you can train your body to relax physically whenever you want. One of the simplest methods to achieve a physically relaxed state is to concentrate on relaxing muscles.

Several acting teachers and a speech teacher have taught me this technique. I have read instructions in texts and listened to audio materials that teach this method. One word of caution before you start. As you cause tension in your muscles, you do not want to strain so hard that you cause damage, nor do you want to strain so hard that you create a muscle cramp. The other thing I should warn you about is that you may fall asleep; after all, it is a relaxation exercise. The basic process goes like this:

> Lie down on your back with your feet slightly separated and your hands placed to your sides. Start with one foot. Point your toes away from your body. Point them until they feel stretched out.

Point them until you can feel the muscle tension in them. Then relax them. Consciously relax them. Do the same with the other foot. Now, back to the first foot, point your toes to your chin until you feel the stretch, then consciously relax. Do the same with the other foot. Next, point your toes far to the right and relax, then far to the left and relax. After you have done all the stretching and relaxing on both feet, concentrate for a moment on how your feet feel. They should feel relaxed. If they do not, do the exercise again.

Now, mentally move up to the calf of one leg. Consciously tighten up the calf muscle and then relax. Repeat with the other calf, then concentrate on your calf muscles. Do they feel relaxed? How about your feet? Are they still relaxed?

Now, do the same with your knees, thighs, buttocks, stomach, chest, shoulders, upper arms, lower arms, hands, neck, jaw, brow, and so on. Your goal is to work your way through every muscle in your body, consciously bringing it to a tense state and then consciously relaxing it. When you are done, your whole body should feel relaxed.

Some people simply need to learn what "relaxed" feels like before they can consciously and instantly choose to relax the whole body. Some people learn where they tend to carry tension through this process. I carry tension in my shoulders. If I want to choose to physically relax, I start with my shoulders. Once I have got my shoulders relaxed, it is fairly easy to make the rest of my body go along.

A Mental Calm

"I can relax my body instantly," Kay said. "I can be a jellyfish at a moment's notice." Kay, who had enrolled in my improvisation class, was a skilled dancer and in complete command of her body. "But I can't stop my mind. It seems like there is always a whirlwind of ideas and thoughts and images in my mind that I can't stop. How do I learn to relax my mind?" Relaxing your mind is different than relaxing your body. In Kay's case, because she had such control of her body, it was even harder to relax her mind. If you work your way through the process of muscle relaxation described above, you will discover that as you have concentrated on taking care of your body, your mind has come along for the ride. By concentrating on what your body is doing, you have pushed all the other images out of your mind. Concentration is a key to learning to relax your mind.

Meditation is just mental concentration, but you concentrate on something specific: an idea, an image, or a person. When I am trying to get my mind to slow down, I meditate on Psalms 23: "The Lord is my shepherd . . ." I never consciously committed this bit of the Christian Scriptures to memory, but I can recite the whole thing. I repeat the psalm slowly in my mind, seeing the words as if they were appearing on a movie screen. The ideas contained in the passage are comforting, even though death is mentioned. If you are going to meditate to relax your mind, then you should meditate on something comforting. While your favorite lyrics may be sung by a death metal punk band, meditating on images of bloody eyeballs and smashed brains is probably not going to do much to help you mentally relax.

Sometimes it is hard to relax mentally when you are in a heightened emotional state, especially if the emotion is a negative one. For example, if you have a broken heart, or if you are angry with someone, those feelings and the thoughts associated with them can be hard to get beyond. In those instances, it is particularly helpful to have something comforting to concentrate on. Sometimes you can literally take something that is mentally blocking your ability to concentrate out of your mind. If you have an important task you need to do, and you are worried about forgetting to do it, then take a moment and write it down. I used to get mentally uptight when I was an adjunct professor because I had so many classes to keep track of, tests to prepare, and lectures to get ready. I discovered that if I took a few moments late on Friday afternoon and wrote out the schedule for the coming week, I felt like I had the next week under control and could relax a lot more easily over the weekend.

There are numerous books about learning to relax both your body and your mind. While I encourage you to investigate further, I also suggest that you tread cautiously and check out thoroughly all your sources of information in this regard. In the arena of controlling your own mind and body there are some strange ideas being promoted as science and religion.

Just Do It!

Betty was a nontraditional student in an evening public speaking course. She was a person who had had many interesting life experiences and delivered very engaging speeches to the class. Because the entire class was composed of nontraditional older students, they liked to go out after class for something to eat. They invited me along once, and I found myself seated next to Betty. Part way through our meal, she turned to me and said, "You know, Mr. Young, after every one of my major speeches I have gone home and thrown up." I was flabbergasted. She had done well in the class, including her speeches. She had a smooth, calm delivery and seemed like she was very much in control of herself as a public speaker. We covered a lot of information about overcoming the fear of public speaking early in the course. I asked her if she remembered all that content, and she did. She could tell me the main points about how to overcome the fear. So I asked her how she put that content into practice. She confessed that she had not. She knew the material, but she had not used it. My final query was how she managed to stay so calm during her major speeches if she was truly that nervous? She reached into her purse and pulled out a bottle of muscle relaxant. Instead of trying to use the knowledge she had, Betty became dependent on substances to make it through her speeches. Why gain knowledge about how to do something if you are never going to put that knowledge to practical use?

Overcoming the fear of performance must be an active process, just like rehearsal. If you do not engage in the steps you need to take to overcome the fear, then the fear will not be overcome. That seems like a simple idea, but I have seen many students short-circuit the process. It is as if they think that knowing how to overcome the fear is enough and that they do not have to participate in the process. It is like thinking that if you know how to drive a car, then that knowledge alone, without actually driving, will be enough to get you where you are going.

As you plan out your rehearsal process, include the activities you will engage in to overcome the fear of performance. Keep a journal about how you are approaching the fear, how you feel about it as you go through the rehearsal process, how it changes as you near the actual performance. Remember, of course, that the rehearsal itself is also part of the process of overcoming the fear.

Chapter 9

Techniques of the Heart

Creatively Creating Performance, Part II

"How do you act?" It was Liz's constant question. She persistently asked it of her performance professors, and their answers never satisfied her. She wanted to learn how to perform in the same manner you would learn how to tie shoes or change a tire. She expected there to be an unchanging, learnable process she could follow, and when she needed to perform, she would follow that process and achieve her goal.

Art is not like that. Whether it is acting, dancing, painting, sculpting, writing, or whatever, there are no formulas for its creation. But if you are interested in performing, there are some tools you can develop. Your voice and your body are obvious tools. Less obvious is your ability to concentrate and your creativity quotient.

The Care and Feeding of Your Voice

Mark planned on making his living as a preacher. Preachers, of course, use their voices continually. Their voice is how they make their living, how they do their work. So Mark was understandably concerned when his speech professor told him that it sounded like he had nodules on his vocal folds. I had never thought about it before, but for as long as I knew Mark, his voice did sound a little bit like he talked underwater. He went to a laryngologist, who put a couple of fiber optic cables up through his nose and down into his throat. One of the cables provided light; the other was hooked up to a camera. Sure enough, there on Mark's vocal folds were a series of nodules: bumps that affected the clear functioning of his voice. Thankfully, Mark's nodules were not cancerous. It was a simple operation to have them scraped off, and when his vocal folds had healed, there was an amazing new clarity to his voice. Most of us do not think much about our voices, how they work,

93

how to take care of them, and how to make them stronger, but performers cannot afford to be lackadaisical about their voices.

In your throat, the vocal folds are two flaps of tissue that form a V-shaped opening in your larynx. It is that protrusion we call an "Adam's apple." When you breathe without talking, the vocal folds remain relaxed as the air flows through the V-shaped space between them. When you speak, your vocal folds tighten up and come together, filling up the V-shaped space. Then as air passes between them, they vibrate, creating sound. That sound changes by how tight or loose your vocal folds are, and how quickly or slowly they vibrate. The sound further changes by what you do with your lips and tongue before the sound leaves your mouth.

Your vocal folds are living tissues, and you need to care for them just like the rest of your body. Have you ever yelled so much that it hurt your throat? It was your vocal folds that you hurt. You can overwork your vocal folds and cause them to be sore, to swell, and even to tear. Also, when you are sick, they may swell and become incapable of producing sound. When you drink or eat something that is cold, or breathe in cold air, you cause your vocal folds to tighten up in a contraction reaction against the cold. That, too, causes them to be less effective. You need to be aware of how your vocal folds feel. If your throat hurts, take it easy with your voice. If it is cold out, try to keep your throat warm. If the sound of your voice changes, then it is time to go to the laryngologist and have your vocal folds checked.

Because your vocal folds are living tissues, you can strengthen them. The vocal folds of an opera singer can produce sound much more vigorously and for much longer periods of time, without damage, than the vocal folds of the average person. The opera singer's vocal folds gained those capabilities by exercise, much like you would exercise to gain muscle strength.

There are books and websites that can do a much better job of teaching you how to strengthen your voice than I can in the space of this text. If you are a performance major at a college or university, then you are probably required to take a voice class for that purpose. My favorite book in this regard is *Make Your Voice Heard* by writer and animation director Chuck Jones. Jones lays out an easy-to-learn set of exercises that will better your voice and your ability to use your voice.

Body Matters

Your body is obviously the other performance tool you possess. Many texts have been written and university courses taught about how to be aware of your body and how to control it as a performer. Having a performance-ready body does not mean that you must have the physique of an athlete. If we all looked like the lifeguards on *Baywatch*, then who would perform the roles designed for balding, overweight, old men? While being physically fit is a worthwhile, even life-extending goal, being aware of and in control of your body for performance purposes is a different matter.

When you perform, you need to know what your body is doing and how that affects the audience. Frequently, I will point out to actors how their feet are pulling focus, how they are positioned in such a way that they draw the audience's eyes down away from the face. For a young actor to play a senior citizen is difficult, but I have seen it done many times successfully, and it is all in body control. If you can move like an old person moves, stand like an old person stands, then the audience will believe you are old. It is all in how you control your body. As with your voice, it would take another textbook to deal with all the aspects of learning to control your body for performance purposes.

Do Not Think of a Purple Cow

Now that you are thinking of a purple cow, see how long you can hold that image in your mind. Try to see the details. Like most of us, you probably cannot keep the image there for very long before other images and thoughts try to edge their way into your mind. It is all a matter of your ability to concentrate.

Concentration is the ability to focus your mental processes on an activity, or image, or thing. *Good performers can concentrate well on performing.* As a performer, you will do well to build your ability to concentrate and to learn to concentrate as an act of will.

All of us have the ability to concentrate intently, especially when we must. My brother-in-law took me rock climbing, and I found myself seriously concentrating. As I looked down between my legs and saw the ground several hundred feet below me, I concentrated hard on one thing: hanging on to the rocks. I call that involuntary concentration. When your life is threatened, you do not have to try to concentrate, nor choose to concentrate, because you naturally concentrate on saving your life. Life-threatening situations demonstrate to us that we are capable of intense concentration.

There are many good Shakespearean actors who can play *Hamlet* one night, *King Lear* the next, and *Macbeth* the night after. In fact, they not only memorize their own lead roles, but they also know all the lines of the other actors. I have seen actors who can perform the entire Book of Revelation from the Bible, and others who can recite a two-hour long version of *A Christmas Carol*. Have you seen the final episode of *Roots*, in which the lead character finally finds the old African man who can speak the entire history of his tribe, even though it takes several hours to do so? How can these people perform these incredible feats of memory? It is all in being able to concentrate.

We, the people of these United States, are concentration poor. Our daily activities do not require intense concentration, so we do not exercise that ability. Consequently, we begin to lose that ability. One of the key benefits of memorizing something is how it increases your ability to concentrate. But when was the last time you had to memorize something? I cannot think of the last time this was required of me. It was probably the lines for a small role in a play some years back. Most schools no longer require students to memorize anything, save for maybe multiplication tables.

Watching television, videos, and films takes absolutely no concentration on your part. Studies have shown that you are far more likely to fall asleep when you are watching television than when you are reading. The sad truth is that most of us spend hours watching television, and our ability to concentrate has suffered for it.

Even the simple activity of reading enhances your ability to concentrate, but it, too, is a waning activity in our culture. When was the last time you read a book cover to cover just for pleasure? I often ask that question of my freshman classes. Rarely do more than half a dozen hands go up in response. I have even heard students proclaim how they "hate to read."

Want to test your ability to concentrate? Imagine a pure, white block of solid ivory that has been dipped in black paint. Now imagine that someone has cut through the painted block, twice horizontally and twice vertically, and then twice vertically again, only perpendicular to the first vertical cuts. After all the slicing, each side of the cube will look like a tic-tac-toe board. So now what you have is a pile of smaller cubes still in the shape of the larger original cube. How many of those smaller cubes will have one black side, two black sides, three black sides, no black sides? See if you can figure that all out in your head without drawing a diagram or writing anything down. The correct answers appear below.

Although we have lost some of our ability to concentrate, it is not an irreversible loss. There are many activities you can engage in to rebuild your ability to concentrate and to keep it strong. Are you taking a literature class? Take the time to memorize a few poems, or at least a few lines from one. In my theater literature classes, as a student, I would always memorize lines from the plays we were reading and then find ways to use those lines in the long essay exams we took. My professors were always impressed, and I am sure it helped my grade. Try to memorize a passage of Scripture. I work from a Christian worldview and have memorized portions of the Sermon on the Mount several times. I memorize it, then it slips away, and I memorize it again. As a performer it can be fun to memorize some of the more well-known Shakespearian soliloquies. What comes after "To be or not to be? That is the question?" See if you can memorize the names of everyone in your dorm. I knew a student who made it his goal every year to learn the names of everyone in his school. It was only about five hundred students but quite a feat, nonetheless. Become one of the "book people" from Ray Bradbury's novel *Fahrenheit 451* and memorize a whole book. I know, you think that sounds crazy, but it can be done, and you will be amazed at what it does for your mind. Memorize new words to increase your vocabulary. Try to work the new words into conversation. Whatever you choose to memorize, the act will improve your ability to concentrate.

Meditation will also help increase your ability to concentrate. See how long you can hold an image in your mind before it starts to degrade or before other images creep in. Think of someone you know well and see how much detail you can remember about her face. Take one of the pieces you have memorized and see if you can run the words through your mind like a moving caption.

Learn to play chess, or any of the tougher, strategic board games. Do crossword puzzles. Play Twenty Questions. Spell words alphabetically in your mind—that is, "dog" as "dgo," "cat" as "act," "elephant" as "aeehlnpt."

Stop watching TV and turn that time over to reading. Make it your goal for the four years you are in college to read your way through the library, as opposed to one student I knew whose goal was to visit every bar in town at least once a week.

This is an exercise I do with my acting students to help them build concentration: Put their hands behind their backs, then hand them a small object, say a ring of keys. They feel the keys. Take the keys and then put a ball in their hands. They feel the ball. Then, while still holding the ball, they try to remember what the keys felt like. Then take the ball and put a pen in their hands. Holding the pen, they try to remember what the keys felt like and then what the ball felt like and so on. There are thousands of ways to improve your concentration. Investigate some and get to work.

Answers to the block of ivory concentration exercise: There are six cubes with one black side, twelve cubes with two black sides, eight with three black sides, and one with no black sides. If you did not get all that correct, it does not mean that you cannot concentrate, because the exercise involves more than concentration. Whether you got it right or not, if you are serious about performing, then you should work on building your ability to concentrate, so you can apply that ability to performing.

Imagine Something You Have Never Seen Before

It is kind of hard to do, is it not? Whatever you imagine, it is a compilation of shapes, colors, and actions you have seen before. When Mozart composed, he did not create new notes, he created new sequences and new combinations of notes; he created music that was never heard before. When Picasso painted, he did not create new colors or new shapes, but he put colors and shapes into new combinations; he created images that were never seen before. When comedians tell a new joke, they do not create new words or use new syntax; they create new arrangements of words. They create sentences that were never spoken before.

Excellent performers, like all excellent artists, are creative people. While creativity is hard to define, most people recognize it when they see it. Also, most people are creative to one degree or another. I once knew a woman who insisted that she was not creative, but she could make a German chocolate cake that still lives in my dreams. It seems like a simple thing, but she put the ingredients together in a way that surpassed all others.

Some years ago, I spent time as a DJ at a small college radio station. I was on the air for about ten hours a week, and unbeknownst to me, I developed a following. I had a lot of fun, and the on-air time was a great outlet for creative musings. After I had been on the air for a couple of months, a colleague asked me if I would spend some time with the new group of student DJs and teach them how to be creative. I told him that I would gladly spend time with the students, but that I did not think I could teach them anything, because it seemed to me that creativity is not a learnable skill. On the other hand, everyone is capable of being creative and that creativity can be *developed*. I suggested to my colleague that we work on developing these students' creativity by exposing them to the work of creative people and by challenging them to be creative.

Go spend a few evenings at the local improvisational comedy club. Watch actor Robin Williams's movies. Read the newspaper comics every day. Read fiction. Read the biographies of the world's greatest problem solvers—the inventors, the statesmen, and the scientists who altered the course of history by way of creative solutions. Go to the art museum. Go to a ballet, a play, an opera, or the circus. Read poetry. Join the writer's club, the drama club, the Art Student Society.

Another means of growing your creative abilities is to take on creative challenges, do things that force you to think creatively, or engage in activities that make you think outside the box. Go to the hardware store and do not leave until you create a new game and buy all the components to play it. Limit yourself to ten dollars, invite some friends along, and create as a team. Write a poem, a play, a novel. Even if it is bad, your creative ability is stretched in the process. Take your ten dollars and your creative team back to the hardware store. This time your goal is to create a sculpture that moves. Take an art class. Take a performance class. Join the choir. Do anything to break the routine of your normal day: eat breakfast food for dinner, sleep the other way around in your bed, walk backward for ten steps out of every hundred, speak to everyone you see, dress up for no reason. One of my recent New Year's resolutions was to write a short (seriously short) play every day for a year. That year my abilities as a writer were stretched. It was good for me. There are a zillion and one things you can do to enhance your creative ability, but they will only help if you choose to purposefully engage in them.

One final suggestion on developing creativity: Keep a serendipity-oh-wow-hmmm journal. In your serendipity-oh-wow-hmmm journal you keep a record of any events, thoughts, people, occurrences, discoveries that are serendipitous and cause you to mentally or vocally say "oh wow," or give you reason to ponder "hmmm." These events or ideas can be anything. I remember an "oh wow" moment when a big spider walked across the inside of my windshield. First, I was impressed that a spider could hang on to glass, and second, I had an "imitate an animal" assignment in acting class that I had not prepared for yet, so watching the spider became my homework. I had a "hmmm" moment in the shower one day when it occurred to me that the water for my shower came from somewhere, and how incredible it was that my way of life included water from a tap right inside my house, and how the molecules of water in my shower had been around for a long time, and may have been part of the ocean once, or inside a whale, or in a tear— you get the idea. Serendipity-oh-wow-hmmm moments are *not* moments you generate. They happen by chance. You record them to remember the effect they had on you, to make that effect last longer, to recall that effect, and hopefully to cause the event to work its magic on you one more time.

Chapter 10

Here Is a Novel Idea

Performing Prose Fiction

THE FIRST THING I WANT TO DO FOR YOU in this section is to define the genre prose fiction. The best definition of "prose" goes something like this: "Prose is not poetry." That is not a direct quote from any particular dictionary, but it is a definition of "prose" that I found everywhere I looked. Prose is the language of everyday life. Novels, short stories, e-mail, technical manuals, textbooks, letters, term papers, essays, and almost everything else you read and write in a day are in the form of prose. Prose does not have rhythm or meter. Prose may include poetic devices such as metaphors and similes. It may include dialogue. Newspapers and magazines are written in prose.

Prose is classified as fiction or nonfiction. Definitions of "fiction" include this: "Fiction is not fact." Again, this is not a quote from any particular definition, but it is the general idea. *Fiction* involves imagined circumstances. Fiction is an invention of the writer. Fairy tales are fiction. Novels and short stories are fiction. Play and movie scripts are fiction. Sure, these genres are sometimes based in fact but even so they are fiction. Take, for example, a historical novel. I could write a novel about a soldier in the Civil War who fought in the Battle of Gettysburg. The Civil War is fact, the Battle of Gettysburg is fact, but the novel as a whole remains fiction, an invention.

So then "prose fiction" is not poetry, and it is not fact. A novel is prose fiction; a newspaper article is not. A short story is prose fiction; a movie script is not. (Scripts are their own genre of literature.) Sometimes prose fiction takes on the attributes of nonfiction work, but it remains fiction. John Updike's novel *S.* is prose fiction but is written in the form of a series of letters. The author of the letters, the people she is writing to, and thus the letters themselves are all fabrications, not real.

Selecting the Prose Fiction Piece

If you have read novels and short stories all your life, then you probably will not have trouble thinking of a prose fiction piece you want to perform. In this case you will probably want to choose a passage from a favorite novel. If you are not someone who reads much fiction, then go to the library and look for anthologies of short stories. The beauty of looking for your prose fiction passage in short stories is that while it may take you a few days to read a novel, you can read the whole short story in an evening or less. Granted, you can take a passage from a novel you have not finished reading, but it is far better to know the whole of the story. Knowing the whole story will influence the performance choices you make. Suppose you do a passage from a novel about a man who is checking out a small town. Your passage describes how he meets and interacts with people as he learns their customs and manners. If you do not know that the real reason he is in town is to rob the local bank, then your lack of knowledge is going to hurt your performance. It is far better to know the whole of the work you are performing, so short stories are an attractive option for the student who does not have a background in prose fiction reading.

After you choose the piece from which you want to take your passage, you must decide on the passage itself. The simplest method of arriving at your choice is to select some of the more exciting or interesting parts of the piece and try them out.

Selecting an exciting, interesting passage is not hard to do. All it takes is common sense. The long rambling description about the way the town looks at sunset may be an important mood-setter for the novel, but for a performance choice, you want to do much more than set a mood. Whether it is prose fiction, a play, or a movie, the elements that keep our interest are the characters and the actions the characters take. So if you choose a passage that tells of an interesting character engaged in an interesting action, then you are well on your way to an interesting performance.

A character can be interesting for a lot of reasons: the way they act, the way they look, the way they talk, the way they think, or their motivations. The things that make a character interesting may not be the obvious things. At first appearance, Mark Twain's Tom Sawyer is not all that interesting. He is just a kid living with his aunt. But the way he can get other people to do things, the way he justifies his actions to himself, the way he hides his actions from his aunt, the things he thinks about the adult world, are what make him interesting. All real people are interesting. All real people have an infinite depth of character, with a zillion thoughts and bits of knowledge and experiences and beliefs that make them unique individuals. A character in a novel, play, or movie is not infinite. Yes, those characters, if they were real, would have infinite depth, but they do not exist in real life. We only know what the author chooses to tell us. Thus, we can know everything there is to know about those fictional characters. Of course, the good authors try to give us the most interesting bits and pieces. Part of our job as performers is to bring those characters to life, as if they had infinite depth, while only showing the audience the most interesting bits.

Characters make internal actions in their minds and hearts that are just as interesting as the actions we see with our eyes. Actions are the results of the choices the characters make. Sometimes the choices themselves are an interesting action. Performing a passage about a character who decides to confront an enemy can be as interesting as the passage that describes the actual confrontation.

The decisions leading to your choice about what part of a prose fiction piece to perform are as much a part of your heart as your head. You may not be able to delineate in words what makes a passage exciting and interesting—you just know that it is, and that is okay. As you perform, your audience will respond emotionally and cognitively.

Cut the Cutting

The *cutting* you choose may be one long section of prose fiction, or it may be several shorter sections you string together, leaving the in-between parts out. You may choose the latter for the sake of coherence. Whatever the case, you want to cut your selection with a concern for not telling what you can show. This specifically applies to descriptions of paralanguage.

Suppose part of the selection is, "'Look out, the bear is behind you!' Bill shouted." If it is otherwise clear to the audience that it is Bill who speaks, then you do not need the phrase, "Bill shouted." It is a far better choice simply to shout the line, "Look out, the bear is behind you!" The same would hold true for a phrase like, "He laughed." It is better to perform the laughing than to describe it.

The goal of cutting your selection is to keep the action moving. Again, remember that the action may be mental as well as physical. A novelist can take the time to create a mood, build an atmosphere, dig into all the little details. One popular and successful author of horror novels is known to take a page or two to describe a blade of grass. While it works in the novel, as a performance piece it does not do much.

It Is Called a "Picture" Book for a Reason

Sometimes I will have students choose children's literature as one of their prose fiction pieces. If it is what the elementary teachers call a "chapter book," like a regular adult novel but aimed at youth, that is okay. But occasionally students will choose a picture book as their prose fiction piece. Their choice is usually despite my instructions not to do so. They typically try to perform the piece as a normal prose fiction work, and because most picture books have very few words on each page, they spend most of their time turning pages instead of performing. Or in the worst-case scenario, the student tries to use the pictures as part of the performance. The pictures, of course, are too small for the audience to see, and it is awkward and performance-killing to try to hold the book so that the audience can see while simultaneously performing. This is not to say that there is absolutely no place for performing children's picture books, but for now, remember that it is called a "picture" book for a reason.

Chapter 11

To Be or Not to Be

Performing Dramatic Literature (Scripts)

THERE ARE SEVERAL MAJOR DIFFERENCES between the nature of *dramatic literature* and the nature of all other literary genres. The first and most obvious is that the dramatist's main tool is dialogue. Sure, a playwright may narrate some aspects of the play, character descriptions, and character actions, but, with a few rare exceptions, there is more dialogue than anything else in a play script. Writing dialogue that moves the action is not as easy as it may seem. Suppose a character worries about losing his job. The dramatist could have the character say, "I'm worried about losing my job." That works, but suppose the character is dominated by his wife and is under pressure from her to get a raise and a promotion at work. How does the playwright get the character to express his fear of job loss when the character is in conversation with his wife? Not so easily done.

The second and less obvious difference between dramatic literature and other genres is that the dramatist has a different intent for the final product. The ultimate goal of the playwright differs from the poet's goal, the novelist's goal, or the nonfiction writer's goal. The poet, novelist, and nonfiction writer want their works to be read and appreciated. The dramatist, however, wants her work performed. The dramatist intends for a performer or group of performers to stage the work for an audience. The dramatist expects directors and actors and designers to add to the work and make it so much more than just the words in the script. According to playwright Herb Gardner, what he writes is only about 25% of the performance. Gardner expects actors and directors to put back the 75% that is not in the script. Dramatists expect performers to make more of the work. But what the dramatist intends is not an oral interpretation performance. The dramatist does not envision her work being performed by a lone performer with script in hand. The oral interpretation performance of dramatic literature is less than what the author intended as the final product.

Because of the use of dialogue and the intent for performance, dramatic literature has one other difference when compared to prose. Dramatic literature is a work of brevity when compared to most novels. With a few exceptions, most plays can be read in an hour or two and performed in the same time frame. When I wrote papers for English literature classes, I always focused my efforts on a play if I had the choice. I knew I could read a play in an hour or two, but a novel would take me several evenings. Because of this need for brevity, playwrights tend to get right to the point. The action is right now. In the best plays, the story constantly unfolds. Each new line brings new information, new insight, new revelations. Again, it is important to remember that the action may be internal as well as external, and often the playwright cannot display the internal actions of her characters in an obvious manner.

Scene Books

When you need to select a piece of dramatic literature for an oral interpretation performance, one good source is scene books. A scene book is a collection of passages from plays, usually put together for use in acting classes. The scenes are generally categorized according to casting: monologues for males, monologues for females, two men, two women, one man and one woman, two men and one woman. Usually, the scene books will also include a brief synopsis of the whole play. The synopsis is a good place to start but endeavor to read the entire play. You want to portray these characters with all the depth of insight you can, and you will not get full knowledge of the character without reading the whole play. And hey, it will only take you an hour or two to read it.

For your first selection, I suggest you choose something with two characters. If you choose a monologue, then the line between oral interpretation and acting gets seriously fuzzy and hard to distinguish. If you choose three or more characters, then you have a much more difficult time performing the characters in a manner that will allow the audience to keep them separate in their minds.

Split Personality

One of the biggest challenges for the oral interpretation of dramatic literature is keeping the characters separate for yourself and for the audience. (We covered this back in Chapter 5, but here is a quick review.) If you perform a two-person scene between Bill and Bubba, the audience should never become confused as to which of the two is speaking. When Bill speaks, there should be no question in the minds of the audience that it is Bill, and the same holds true for Bubba. The oral interpretation performer has numerous tools at her disposal to help create the illusion of two people talking to each other.

The first tool is called *character placement*, or *character focus*. The oral interpretation performer must decide where she is going to look as she performs. When performing dramatic literature, this decision must be made for each character. Each character must have a particular focus, and that focus, in most cases, should not change in performance.

Take your Bill and Bubba scene for instance, or any two-character scene. Imagine you are standing face to face with someone about two feet away from you. Without changing body position, turn your head and look over that person's left shoulder. When you speak Bill's lines, that is Bill's focus. Now turn and look over the person's right shoulder. When you speak Bubba's lines, that will be Bubba's focus. In simpler terms, you put the focus of one character slightly to the left and the focus of the other slightly to the right. I say "slightly" because if they are too far apart, the turning of your head from side to side becomes comical and calls attention to the act itself. I have seen students place the focus of the two characters so far apart that they were almost in full profile. The performance was more like a gymnastics floor exercise, as the students swung violently from left to right and right to left trying to keep their characters placed in the correct focus. This broad action worked against the performance. Keeping the character foci only slightly apart makes the difference much more manageable and performable.

When you have a third character, you put the focus of one character in the middle, and the other two slightly to the sides. When you have four characters, you put two to the left, with one of them being slightly more to the left than the other, and the same on the right. Personally, I recommend against four characters for the neophyte oral interpretation performer but try it if you must—you may shine.

Another obvious tool to help you keep the characters separate in the minds of the audience is overall body posture. If Bill stands up straight and

Bubba slightly slumps, then the audience can see that difference and can more easily keep the two separated in their minds. Of course, you would not want Bubba to slump if he was not the kind of character who would slump. If Bubba is a spit-and-polish army officer, then slumping would work against your portrayal of him. Body posture can change as little as one character keeping her weight on both feet and one character keeping her weight only on one foot. Any simple thing that is easy to perform and keeps with the nature of the character will help the audience differentiate between the characters.

Your characters can have individualized hand gestures or facial tics or quirky smiles or laughs. Anything and everything that makes up a characterization is fair game for your interpretation and for helping the audience keep characters separate in their minds.

Yet another performance tool to help your audience differentiate between characters is to give each character distinct paralanguage characteristics. Along with all the normal variations in paralanguage that go with changing emotional states, each character can have her own distinct vocal characteristics that are present regardless of other paralanguage changes. A character may tend to have a high-pitched voice or a low one. She may have a slightly hoarse voice, or she may speak in a breathy "starlet" manner. A character may tend to talk slowly or to speak with an oddly paced rhythm. While there are all kinds of vocal idiosyncrasies you can give a character via paralanguage, you want to find something that is right for the character.

A major concern for oral interpretations of dramatic literature is ensuring the audience keeps the characters separate in their minds and knows when each different character speaks. This clarity is achieved by engaging in careful character placement, crafting distinct postures or gestures, and creating distinctive nonverbal qualities for each character.

One final and fun exercise is to rehearse the individual character lines separately. In other words, become Bubba and do all his lines "in character" without doing Bill's lines.

Chapter 12

Holding Someone's Heart

Performing Poetry

THE ORAL INTERPRETATION OF POETRY is one of the more challenging, exciting, interesting, and enjoyable performance genres. Poetry may well be the most paradoxical of all forms of written language. Some poetry, such as haiku, sonnet, and limerick, follow strict formats and rules of composition. Other forms of poetry, such as blank verse and free verse, may not have a particular form or follow any rules of language. A poet may ignore all the standard mechanics of writing—punctuation, capitalization, or grammar. A poem may have lines of varying length with no apparent pattern, or lines that follow distinct patterns of length. Poets are the true adventurers of the written word. They can go anywhere, do anything, ignore or follow syntactical rules, make up their own rules—a poet may even make up her own rules just to violate them.

Poetry is also the purest literary art form, at least in terms of an author's motivation. The best writers of all genres write honestly from their hearts. But novelists, playwrights, short story writers, and especially nonfiction writers all look beyond the moment, hoping for a publication, a production, and a royalty check to arrive in the mail someday. I do not mean to say that these other writers are only motivated by financial gain. Most high-quality writers write because they believe they have something worth saying and they want to say it well. Nevertheless, with other literary forms, there is still the potential for financial reward if all goes well. The best poets, however, are truly and only motivated by the simple yet complex desire to create a moment of significance via words. While I assume that all serious poets hope to be published, I also believe they all are realistic enough to know they are not going to pay their bills via royalty checks from poetry. (I cannot recall the last time I bought a book of poetry simply because I wanted to.) My point here is that most poets write with truly altruistic motives.

So what? What does that have to do with oral interpretation? As I have noted previously, when a performer deals with a literary work, she should have the attitude that she is handling a piece of the author's heart. When you rehearse and perform a poem, that is when you are most likely to come away with some bloodstains (figuratively speaking and meant in a good way).

As with other forms, the first step in creating an oral interpretation of poetry is the selection process, and as with other genres, you want to select the poetry piece with the audience in mind. A good place to begin the selection process is with poetry anthologies. A poet like Carl Sandburg wrote about anything and everything and did so in his own unique style. Or you may want to find anthologies created around a theme or an era. Perhaps you can find *The Best American Poems of the Twentieth Century*, or *Verses from England*, or *Poems Written by Left-Handed Hog Farmers in Iowa* (all fictitious titles, as far as I know). Those kinds of anthologies will give you a greater variety, in form and content, to select from than collected works of any specific author. But either choice is good for its own reasons.

Rhyme and Reason . . . Ableness

Poetic language possess features that are not found in conversational speech. Most specifically, some poems *rhyme*, and most people do not normally speak in rhyme. If you choose a poem that rhymes, one of the key concerns in rehearsal and performance is to prevent the rhyme from ruling the performance of the poem. We all have heard someone read a poem that had a very strong rhyme, and the rhyme was so pronounced that the reading took on a pattern, a rhythm, a cadence that overpowered the rest of the poem. Rhyme is not bad; in fact, it can be delightful. Rhythm, patterns, cadence in a poem—those are not bad either. An author can purposefully create rhythm as an element of the poem. If so, you should want to use that device in the performance. The problem occurs when a rhythm driven by the rhyme takes over the poem. It is as if you cannot hear the poem for the rhyme. Your goal is to make the rhyme seem like a natural non-distracting part of the poem— not hidden, but not calling attention to itself either.

One way to help overcome the tendency to stress the rhyme is to write the poem out in paragraph form, not in stanzas. A reason we tend to stress the rhyme is that the rhyming words fall at the end of the lines but not necessarily at the ends of the sentences. A sentence in a poem can end anywhere in a line. By rehearsing the poem from a draft that is written out in paragraph form, you will naturally add the normal pauses between sentences. You will, in a manner of speaking, read the punctuation, not the rhyme.

This problem is complicated by a rhymed poem that does not have any punctuation. In that case, it is helpful to add punctuation of your own to overcome the tendency to emphasize the rhyme. Once the rhyme is conquered, the added punctuation must be removed.

Because some poetry is confined to a certain length or format—for example, a sonnet or a haiku—you will have to decide how the format will affect the performance. You may want to stress the shortness of the lines of a haiku and make the shortness part of the impact of the performance. You may want to stress the form of the sonnet and make that form part of the performance.

Some classic forms of poetry have a rhythm built into the form that involves the stressed accents of the words. You should investigate the nature of that rhythm and explore whether to make it an overt part of the performance.

Your poem may not have punctuation, or it may use punctuation in unusual ways. If the poem has no punctuation, then you will want to perform the poem as if it did, with natural pauses where they feel right. If the poem has punctuation, especially if it is used in abnormal ways, then you want to pay particular attention to it, since the author put it there for a reason.

Figures of Speech

Poetry tends to use figures of speech far more often than other forms of creative writing. Most students will have considered the major figures of speech in an English literature class, but I will provide a brief review here:

A **metaphor** makes a direct comparison: "Her eyes were limpid pools of motor oil."

A **simile** uses "like" or "as" in the comparison: "Her eyes were like limpid pools of motor oil."

Personification assigns human qualities to animals or inanimate objects: "The wise owl played Mozart on the stoic piano."

Hyperbole is exaggeration: "In the morning he felt like a thousand gorillas had danced on his tongue all night."

Onomatopoeia is a word that sounds like the thing it means: "Buzz," "whirrrrrr," "bang," "boom."

Synecdoche substitutes a part for the whole: "He called the hand on deck." ("Hand" equates to a whole sailor from head to toe.)

Metonymy substitutes the whole with something associated with it. The most famous example of metonymy is, "The pen is mightier than the sword." "Pen" stands for the written word and "sword" stands for physical acts of aggression.

There are other figures of speech, but these are the most taught in English classes.

Does knowing about the figures of speech help you perform? Not necessarily. Do authors think in terms of figures of speech as they write? Probably not! So why is it useful to know about these devices? It helps you to understand how artistic language is used. For you, it may be most important to remember that it is one thing to identify figures of speech and a different thing to perform them well.

Accessibility

One final thing to consider when performing poetry is the accessibility of the poetry to the typical audience member. By *accessibility* I mean the degree to which a person will understand the meaning of the poem. I do not mean to suggest that a good poem must be easy to understand—in fact, some of the best poems are the most obscure—but because of the special nature of poems, because of the special way poets use language, you want to consider how readily the audience will understand the poem and adjust your performance accordingly.

Chapter 13

A Soup-Can Label Is Nonfiction

Performing Nonfiction Prose

MY FIRST ORAL INTERPRETATION PROFESSOR was a fun man. We had a good time in his class and learned a lot. Our last assignment was to perform a three-to-five-minute piece from any genre we wanted, and to try something different—to take a risk and do something unusual. So for my piece, I performed a soup-can label. I copied all the words from a soup can into manuscript format, then rehearsed and performed them as if they were a deeply dramatic reading—what we might call "melodrama." It mildly amused the audience, and I got an A for most unusual source. When I confessed that I was not sure which genre a soup-can label would be, Mr. Johnson wryly stated that a soup-can label would be nonfiction prose.

Anything that is not made up, make-believe, or a falsehood is *nonfiction*. Opinion essays, news articles, diaries, journals, letters, and true adventure stories are all nonfiction. While nonfiction is not the most obvious choice of genre for oral interpretation, it works well. The success you will or will not have performing a nonfiction piece depends on all the same things for performing any other genre. If you pick an interesting passage and perform it well, then your nonfiction oral interpretation will be a success.

One thing to consider as you explore and rehearse a nonfiction piece is the intent of the author. Sure, you should consider that with all genres, but it is something you want to think a little more about when you perform nonfiction.

Most often, *diaries* are never meant to be read by anyone other than the author. Diaries are certainly not meant to be performed by anyone in a public setting. But because some diaries, especially those of famous people, are so interesting, they get published and read. As a performer, you must decide how the intimacy of a personal diary will affect your performance. Do you want to maintain a mood that would suggest the author is talking to herself or to perform the piece as if the audience and you were both part of the author's psyche?

While journals are similar to diaries, they are sometimes written with the intent of being read by someone else. This is especially true of journals written for the purpose of reporting—for example, the journals of the Lewis and Clark Expedition. While the Lewis and Clark journals contain many personal reflections, both men knew that the journals would be read by the government officials to whom they would eventually report. Beyond that, some journals are written with the idea of publication for public consumption in the author's mind at the time of writing. This is especially true of real-life adventure stories that take the form of a journal. If you choose to perform a passage from a journal, then you will need to learn the circumstances surrounding the creation of that journal and decide how that knowledge will influence your performance choices.

Letters are obviously meant to be read by at least one other person but rarely intended for more than one. But like diaries, the letters of famous people are often so interesting that some scholar or historian will collect them together and publish them. For example, I have the published version of John Steinbeck's letters. It is over a thousand pages long, and contains only a portion of all the letters he wrote. If you choose to perform letters, then you want to think about what stage of the letter you wish to perform. Will your performance represent the creation of the letter? Will you be the mind of the author as she puts these thoughts on paper? Or will you be the recipient of the letter? Will your performance choices reflect the feelings of the recipient as she discovers the content of the letter? Or will your performance reveal some other aspect of the letter, the author, or the recipient?

Sometimes a newspaper article makes a wonderful piece for oral interpretation, but you must remember that good journalists are supposed to report the facts without putting a spin on them. A good passage from a newspaper for the purposes of oral interpretation is a section that holds interesting facts reported in interesting language. Years ago, I performed an oral interpretation of a newspaper article about a panel of experts that had decided Santa Claus was a fraud who caused children to be greedy. Besides being a fun story, it contained lots of quotes from the various people involved, and so I could create a character voice and posture for each of them.

The Essay

You are probably reading this text in an academic setting and are therefore likely familiar with the *essay*. In fact, most of you have probably written your fair share as homework. Essays are composed of structured writing that usually occurs in an academic setting and serves one of three purposes: essays are descriptive, evaluative, or argumentative. Essays can serve other purposes, but careful analysis will find that an essay fits into one of the above categories. All this, however, does not mean that an essay must be dry and lacking in entertainment value. Jonathan Swift's famous essay *A Modest Proposal* is a satirical poke at the attitudes of the rich toward the poor.

When you choose material from an essay as your nonfiction oral interpretation performance, you would do well to figure out which category of purpose your choice fits. You would also do well to either pick a topic you feel strongly about or to pick something that is quite entertaining—or both.

A Final Word

One final word of warning about performing nonfiction. Make sure it *is* nonfiction. Some fiction takes on the form of nonfiction. Daniel Defoe's *Robinson Crusoe* is fiction in the form of a journal. Alice Walker's *The Color Purple* and John Updike's *S.* are in the form of a collection of letters, but both are fiction. If your class assignment is nonfiction, make sure your passage meets the genre requirements.

Chapter 14

"I Get By with a Little Help from My Friends"

Group Performance—Reader's Theater and Choral Reading

SOMETIMES READER'S THEATER IS CALLED "Theater of the Mind" because much of the performance takes place in the audience's mind. Theater theorists kick around an idea called "suspension of disbelief," which is mentioned previously in this book. In simple terms, *suspension of disbelief* means that the audience is willing to ignore the fact that all the action and dialogue on stage are not real, that it is all pretend, that it is all false. The audience chooses to ignore that fact and to engage in the drama in a vicarious fashion. That combination of ignoring and engaging is the suspension of disbelief. Reader's theater asks the audience members to suspend their disbelief to a much higher degree than regular theater. When you view a play, there is the attempt to create verisimilitude—something appearing to be real even though it is not. When you view a reader's theater, there is no attempt at verisimilitude. In a good reader's theater performance, actions are suggested by body movements and characters are posed via nonverbal communications, but none of that happens to the extent that it does in a full theater production of a play.

Simply put, reader's theater is a group performance of literary material wherein each performer engages in oral interpretation, not acting. Understand that this is a very broad definition with lots of shades of gray. When actor Patrick Stewart does his one-man performance of Dickens's *A Christmas Carol*, is it a play or is it reader's theater? He does not hold a script, so it could be called a play. On the other hand, he works from Dickens's original novel, not a script version of the work, so it could be oral interpretation. The point is that we all know a play when we see one, and we all know oral interpretation when we see it, but there is no absolute, clearly marked delineation between the two.

The uses of reader's theater are many, and there are no limitations on who to use as performers. It is a wonderful way to get children of all ages to perform together without nearly as much rehearsal time as you need for a play. Classes of all ages can be transmogrified into a reader's theater group. The performers are much less fearful of the performance as they have no lines to memorize. The teacher or director has far less work than producing a play. The only real requisite would be the ability to read aloud. Although, there are some reading pedagogies that can incorporate reader's theater into the process of learning to read.

Reader's theater is a wonderful mode of performance for the church or civic group that has limited rehearsal time. With so many churches adding drama to their repertoire of fine arts, reader's theater is the ideal place to start. Want to start doing some drama with your senior citizen group? Reader's theater may be the answer.

Personally, I have been engaged in reader's theater in educational settings from elementary school through my postgraduate work. Apart from school, I have directed or performed reader's theater for churches and community theaters. One of my favorite uses was the Christmas performance of our Summer Repertory Theater at Blackburn College. (The Christmas performance of a summer theater may be the world's best oxymoron.) I like to use reader's theater in that venue because everyone is very busy at that time of year and rehearsal time is limited. While the actual rehearsal schedule depends on the cast and the script, I can usually get between eight and a dozen rehearsals and come up with a pretty good show.

Reader's theater is great for neophyte performers. It is a good way to get them in front of an audience without taking on a whole play. It is also a good way to get them interested enough in performing so that they move on to full plays.

Reader's theater scripts can come from all the same sources as any other oral interpretation material. One of the simplest ways to put together a reader's theater production is to use a regular play script and perform it as reader's theater instead of as a play. (See Appendix B about rights and royalties.) You may take a novel and shorten it into a reader's theater or perform the whole of a short story. I have performed in reader's theaters that pulled together bits and pieces of literature from a variety of sources all thematically connected. The title of one piece was *We Like It Here, But,* and we put it together in a reader's theater workshop at California State University, Hayward in the early 1970s. The piece was about the foibles and fortes of living in America during that time. It included material from humor magazines, newspapers, academic journals, novels, popular song lyrics, plays, and a few things we wrote ourselves.

I have seen and performed in reader's theater that used nothing more than an empty stage. I have also engaged in reader's theater that had a simple set: platforms and boxes. It might be a mistake to have a full-blown, realistic set for a reader's theater piece if the set specifically depicts a place for the action of the drama, but this is art, so take the risk. Suppose I did *A Christmas Carol* as a reader's theater and put the cast in a place that looked like Scrooge's office or his bedroom or Cratchit's living room—would that be a mistake? Suppose I created a set that looked like a back alley of London and simply let that be the setting for the reader's theater? That can work well, too.

Costumes, like sets, depend largely on what effect you want to create. For our summer theater's Christmas show, I had all my performers wear at least one winter garment: a warm hat, muffler, gloves. It gave the effect of winter and Christmas without having performers getting too hot, and it added some color without having to worry about designing specific costumes.

Props depend on what you are trying to create, as well. We did a piece last Christmas about a guy who received socks as a Christmas present, and it worked to have a prop involved. But he was the only one to handle it, and we kept it very simple.

I have seen reader's theaters shift too close to acting while remaining reader's theater. One unfortunate performance was a story that included a rape, and the performers tried to reenact the rape scene, script in hand. To see a man and a woman rolling about the floor still grasping their scripts is asking too much of any audience. Unless the intention was comedy, and it was not in this case, no audience would suspend their disbelief to that degree. A much better choice would have been to keep the rape in an oral interpretation mode, with both performers facing the audience, holding their scripts and not even looking at each other. Or if the director wanted the rape enacted, to require them to memorize the lines and abandon the scripts for the rape scene. That would have been jumping from oral interpretation to acting and back again, but that is okay. This is art, and there are no absolute rules, so long as the finished product works for the audience.

In a reader's theater production of *In Search of Eusebius Hershey*, twice I had my performers memorize their lines, abandon their scripts, and fully act out a short scene. In both cases, the scene was an intimate moment. The first was a proposal of marriage, and the second was Eusebius coming home to his wife, who thought he was dead. In both cases, the intimacy of relationships made me think that a fully acted scene would work better. And it did.

Speaking of directors, it is usually a good idea to have one for a reader's theater performance. The director's duties in a reader's theater rehearsal-performance process will vary from situation to situation. Most of the director's duties are the same as in a regular play, though perhaps less demanding. Those duties may include leading the rehearsals and the rehearsal process, giving feedback to actors, staging (blocking) the show, selecting a script, auditioning a cast, supervising technical aspects, and being artistically responsible for the performance. Most directors of plays do an in-depth script analysis before the rehearsal process begins. A director of reader's theater may or may not do that kind of analysis, depending on the circumstances. It is important to remember that the effort to create verisimilitude in a reader's theater is far different than in a play. Generally, a person who can direct a play well will be able to direct a reader's theater well.

Back in the days when I had an annual excursion into directing reader's theater, I was usually responsible for the script selection, casting (which may or may not have included an audition process), staging the show, leading the rehearsal process, and being responsible for the overall aesthetic effect of the performance. I did not usually use a stage manager, and I did not usually do much script analysis. Where I may have thirty rehearsals for a two-act play, I would only have seven to ten for an hour-long reader's theater.

I encourage you to engage in reader's theater wherever you work. Educational, community, and church groups are all prime breeding grounds for the performing arts, and reader's theater is a great place to begin.

Choral Reading

Imagine a choir singing an hour-long work. Sometimes they all sing at once, during other moments, only one voice is heard, and at other moments, a handful of voices, but not the whole choir. *Choral reading* is exactly like that, only it is spoken, not sung.

My first experience with oral interpretation was a choral reading performance. When Mr. K had us read *The Twelve Days of Christmas* as a performance for our parents, he directed us just like a choir, but we were engaged in choral reading. Choral reading, like reader's theater, is easy to produce, fun to engage in, and a great performance vehicle for all kinds of groups.

Producing choral reading is straightforward and simple. Suppose it is Black History Month, and you decide you want to do a choral reading performance of one of Dr. Martin Luther King Jr.'s speeches. Let's say your group is 25 upper elementary school students. You get everyone an easily readable (large font, double-spaced) copy of the speech. Select your strongest reader and have her read the first line loud and clear.

> "I am happy to join you today in what will go down in history as the greatest demonstration for freedom in the history of our nation." When she gets to the phrase "go down in history," have half of the class join her in saying those words. You must rehearse it so that the solo voice does not slow down when she gets to that phrase and the half of the class who join her do so without hesitation. Then have the other half join in for "greatest demonstration of freedom."

The script would look like this:

Solo Voice: I am happy to join you today in what will

Half the Class: go down in history

Solo Voice: as the

Whole Class: greatest demonstration of freedom

Solo Voice: in the history of our nation.

Rehearse that over and over so that once the solo voice starts, the rest of it flows like a normal sentence. Continue to break the speech up into single voices and multiple voices, as you want to add attention and emphasis to certain words or phrases.

Here is an example of a familiar piece fully scripted for a choral reading.

The Pledge of Allegiance to the Flag

One Voice: I pledge

Ten Voices: allegiance

Two Voices: to the Flag

Four Voices: of the United States of America,

Eight Voices: and to the Republic

Four Voices: for which it stands,

All the Male Voices: one Nation

All the Female Voices: under God,

Everyone: indivisible,

Half the Group: with liberty

Other Half: and justice

One Voice: for all.

There are multitudes of things you can do. One of my favorites is to have all the voices join in on only one word in a solo line. Another is to progressively add in voices so that the volume and intensity increase with each word. I have also experimented with subtracting voices so that the intensity and volume decrease.

In the piece about Eusebius Hershey noted above, I had a list of 45 Scripture verses from which Eusebius had preached in as many days. Wanting to expose the audience to his versatility, but not wanting to bore them to death, I divided the list into three parts of 15 verses each. I had one reader start shouting out the verses on her list. Five verses in, a second reader started shouting out the verses on his list. Five verses later, the third reader joined in. So in the middle, for five verses, all three performers were shouting out verses, then it pulled back to two, and finished with one. Granted, the performance was a reader's theater and not a choral reading, but the genre's overlap and a good director will be eclectic enough to creatively use whatever technique works for the piece in question.

Choral reading is a fun, simple, inexpensive way to get neophyte performers involved in performing. I encourage all of you who teach to try it out in your classrooms or elsewhere.

Appendix A

Some Final Thoughts

If It Is Not Fun, You Are Doing It Wrong!

Oral interpretation remains a somewhat obscure art form, but it is one that can be engaged in for an infinite number of reasons in almost any circumstance.

As a classroom tool, it is a magnificent way to get students of all ages to engage with literature of all types.

Oral interpretation is a great way to put together a fundraising performance for any theater group, amateur or professional.

Worship services can be spiced up by an oral interpretation of the day's Scripture. Sermons can be illustrated by a short oral interpretation performance.

Most local talent shows are filled with singers and dancers. Stand out with a comedic passage presented as an oral interpretation performance.

I hope this book is useful to you. Although there are many suggestions above about what you should or should not do in an oral interpretation performance, remember that this is art, and there are no rules. In the final analysis, if the audience walks away entertained, moved, lifted-up, encouraged, challenged, or otherwise touched, then you have been successful.

And have fun! If your oral interpretation work is not fun (even when engaged in heavy dramatic pieces), then you are doing it wrong.

Appendix B

Performance Rights and Royalties

Sometimes people who engage in creating amateur theater are surprised to learn that they need to pay a royalty to produce a play. I recall the story of a first-year high school teacher being pressured into directing the fall play and then having to tell her administration that they would need to come up with the money to buy the scripts and pay the royalties. Apparently, the previous director had illegally ignored all that and produced plays without paying any royalty. They were lucky they did not get caught and fined.

When our summer theater group produced Robert Fulghum's play *Uh-Oh, Here Comes Christmas*, we performed it as a reader's theater, did not sell tickets, and only took donations at the door, but *we paid the requisite royalty*. In that case doing the right thing was simple. It was a published script with a royalty contract.

In other cases, knowing what to do to keep things legal is a bit tougher. When I did a reader's theater of the works of a popular children's poet, I spent some time reading copyright laws and finally contacted the publisher to see if we could legally perform for a nonpaying audience. They never contacted me back, and we proceeded to perform.

I know that in a classroom setting, *with no other audience than the class*, there is no question of needing permission or paying a royalty. So long as it stays in the classroom setting, it is fine.

In other circumstances, the legality can get fuzzy, especially when performing work that was not intended for performance. There are a lot of shades of gray here, and I would encourage you to investigate the "fair use" rules for copyrighted material. There is a good bit of leniency for classroom use, but do not say I did not warn you.

Index